Interface-Oriented Design

Interface-Oriented Design

Ken Pugh

The Pragmatic Bookshelf
Raleigh, North Carolina   Dallas, Texas

Many of the designations used by manufacturers and sellers to distinguish their products are claimed as trademarks. Where those designations appear in this book, and The Pragmatic Programmers, LLC was aware of a trademark claim, the designations have been printed in initial capital letters or in all capitals. The Pragmatic Starter Kit, The Pragmatic Programmer, Pragmatic Programming, Pragmatic Bookshelf and the linking *g* device are trademarks of The Pragmatic Programmers, LLC.

Every precaution was taken in the preparation of this book. However, the publisher assumes no responsibility for errors or omissions, or for damages that may result from the use of information (including program listings) contained herein.

Our Pragmatic courses, workshops, and other products can help you and your team create better software and have more fun. For more information, as well as the latest Pragmatic titles, please visit us at

> http://www.pragmaticprogrammer.com

Printed in the United States of America.

ISBN 0-9766940-5-0

Printed on acid-free paper with 85% recycled, 30% post-consumer content.

First printing, June 2006

Version: 2006-6-19

Dedicated to Nameless II,
the cat who sat on my lap
while I typed this book.

Contents

Preface

Interface-Oriented Design explores how you can develop software with interfaces that interact with each other. We'll look at techniques for breaking down solutions into these interacting interfaces and then for determining appropriate implementations for these interfaces to create well-structured programs. We have plenty of examples that will show you ways to create effective designs composed of interfaces to objects, components, and services. And we'll even have some fun along the way.

You've probably learned about (and experienced) software development using object-oriented design. Interface-oriented design concentrates on the interfaces of modules, which may or may not be implemented with object-oriented languages. Designs that emphasize interfaces are loosely coupled—and that's a good thing. If you have only an interface to which to code, you cannot write code dependent on an implementation, which helps keep us honest.

Distributed computing, such as service-oriented architectures, places a particular emphasis on interfaces. The interfaces may be procedure oriented (such as Remote Procedure Calls) or document oriented (such as web services). We'll explore the transparency and loose coupling traits that are key to distributed interfaces to help you build better distributed systems.

Inheritance is often a tricky technique to get correct—it is often one of the most abused features in object-oriented languages. We'll look at designs that employ inheritance versus ones that emphasize interfaces to demonstrate the trade-offs between the two.

This ongoing emphasis on interfaces may seem a bit extreme. But by looking at one extreme, you'll start to see a different viewpoint that can give you fresh insights into your current approach to software development.

Here then is a road map for our journey through interface-oriented design.

Road Map

Chapter 1, *Introduction to Interfaces*

We'll start by ordering pizza. One should never read a book on an empty stomach, so we'll use the activities of finding a suitable pizza shop and ordering a pizza as a nonprogramming introduction to interfaces. We'll then briefly look at some code and textual interfaces as introductory background for topics we'll explore in later chapters.

Chapter 2, *Interface Contracts*

It's hard to use an interface if an implementation provides no guarantee of working successfully. We'll see how the Three Laws of Interfaces applies to implementations and how Design by Contract helps in understanding an interface's protocol. Finally, you'll need to test an implementation to verify that it lives up to its side of the contract.

Chapter 3, *Interface Ingredients*

You can structure interfaces in many ways, including pull versus push and stateful versus stateless interfaces. We'll explore the trade-offs and benefits of these facets and finish by outlining how to transform an interface from one facet to another.

Chapter 4, *What Should Be in an Interface?*

An interface should have cohesive functionality. There are no absolute rules to what makes a cohesive interface, but we'll look at different sets of interfaces to explore the concept of cohesiveness and see how it helps development.

Chapter 5, *Inheritance and Interfaces*

Inheritance in object-oriented programs is often overused. We'll investigate better ways to organize designs using interfaces and delegation and discover the trade-offs and benefits over inheritance.

Chapter 6, *Remote Interfaces*

Many programs these days are dependent on communicating with remote interfaces. We'll look at the ramifications of using remote interfaces, see why document-style interfaces are becoming more common, and learn how to best organize one.

Chapter 7, *A Little Process*

Interface-oriented design is but one part of the overall development process. We'll see how it fits in, and we'll get ready for the three design examples in the following chapters.

Chapter 8, *Link Checker*

In this chapter, we'll develop a miniproject: a link checker for web pages, demonstrating how interfaces provide flexibility in selecting implementations.

Chapter 9, *Web Conglomerator*

Why rely on web sites to put information together in the way that you want it? The web conglomerator project gathers information into a single page and lets us explore interface cohesiveness and interface generalization as we create this program.

Chapter 10, *Service Registry*

Remote services use directories to help you locate a service provider. In this project, we'll develop a service registry to explore how directory services work and see an example of a document-style interface.

Chapter 11, *Patterns*

The well-known "Gang of Four" book divides patterns into two camps: class-based and object-based. To give another viewpoint, we'll look at some of those classic patterns as being interface-based instead.

Who Should Read This Book

This book is aimed at developers who have some experience with programming and who have been exposed to object-oriented design. Even if you are heavy into object orientation, you might find the interface-oriented approach helps you gain some insight into different ways of approaching a design. Understanding interfaces will help you transition to designing Service-Oriented Architectures.

About the Cover

Concentrating on interfaces is key to decoupling your modules.[1] You probably learned to type on a QWERTY keyboard, as shown on the cover. That interface is the same regardless of whether the implementation is an old-fashioned typewriter, a modern electric typewriter, or a computer keyboard. There have been additions to the keyboard, such as function keys, but the existing layout continues to persist.

But other layouts, such as Dvorak,[2] are more efficient for typing. You can switch your computer keyboard to use an alternate layout; the switching module works as an adapter. Inside the keyboard driver, the keystrokes are converted to the same characters and modifiers (e.g., Shift, Alt, etc.) that are produced by the regular keyboard.

The QWERTY keyboard layout was derived from concern about implementation. According to one web site,[3] "It is sometimes said that it was designed to slow down the typist, but this is wrong; it was designed to allow *faster* typing—under a constraint now long obsolete. In early typewriters, fast typing using nearby type-bars jammed the mechanism. So Sholes fiddled the layout to separate the letters of many common digraphs (he did a far from perfect job, though; *th*, *tr*, *ed*, and *er*, for example, each use two nearby keys). Also, putting the letters of *typewriter* on one line allowed it to be typed with particular speed and accuracy for demos. The jamming problem was essentially solved soon afterward by a suitable use of springs, but the keyboard layout lives on."

Creating interfaces that are easy to use and decoupling their use from their implementation are two facets that we'll explore a lot in this book. (And you may have thought the cover was just a pretty picture.)

So, What Else Is in Here?

Simple Unified Modeling Language (UML) diagrams show the class and interface organization throughout the book. We use Interface-Responsibility-Interaction (IRI) cards, a variation of Class-Responsibility-Colla-

---

[1]As Clemens Szyperski puts it, "The more abstract the class, the stronger the decoupling achieved." See http://www.sdmagazine.com/documents/sdm0010k/.

[2]See http://www.microsoft.com/enable/products/dvlayout.aspx.

[3]See http://www.ctrl-c.liu.se/~ingvar/jargon/q.html.

boration (CRC) cards, as the primary method for creating an interface-oriented designs. You'll also find code examples in multiple languages to show how interfaces are implemented in those languages.

On a terminology note, the OMG Modeling Language Specification (revision 1.3) uses the phrase *realize interface*, which means a component implements the services defined in the interface. Allen Holub in *Holub on Patterns* uses the term *reify*, which means "consider an abstract concept to be real." I thought about alternating one of those verbs with the word *implements*, but they are less familiar. If you get tired of seeing *implementing*, just imagine it's *reify*.

You will see a few sections that look like this:

"Joe Asks..."
These sections provide answers for some common questions.

Acknowledgments

I would like to thank my reviewers for reading the draft copies of this book and contributing numerous comments that helped improve the book. Thanks to David Bock, Tom Ball, Ron Thompson, Gary K. Evans, Keith Ray, Rob Walsh, David Rasch, Carl Manaster, Eldon Alameda, Elias Rangel, Frédérick Ros, J. Hopkins, Mike Stok, Pat Eyler, Scott Splavec, Shaun Szot, and one anonymous reviewer. Thanks to Michael Hunter, an extraordinary tester, who found a lot of "bugs" in this book. Thanks to Christian Gross, a reviewer who gave me many suggestions that just couldn't fit into this book and to Kim Wimpsett for proofreading the manuscript.

I appreciate Andy Hunt, my editor and publisher, for encouraging me to write this book, and all his help with the manuscript.

Thanks also to Leslie Killeen, my wife, for putting up with me writing another book just as soon as I finished my previous book, *Prefactoring*, winner of the 2006 Software Development Jolt Product Excellence Award.[4]

And now, here we go!

---

[4]See http://www.ddj.com/dept/architect/187900423?pgno=3/.

Part I

All about Interfaces

Chapter 1

Introduction to Interfaces

We'll start our introduction to interfaces with ordering a pizza. The pizza order is not just to ensure that reading begins on a full stomach; by using non-computer-related matter, we can explore some general topics relating to interfaces, such as polymorphism and implementation hiding, without getting bogged down in technology. Then we'll switch to real systems to show code and textual interfaces as background for topics in later chapters.

1.1   Pizza-Ordering Interface

If you're a real programmer, or a serious pizza eater, you've probably performed the following scenario hundreds of time.

The Pizza Order

You're hungry so you call your favorite pizza joint.

"Yo," the voice on the other end answers, ever so politely.

"I'd like a large pizza," you reply.

"Toppings?" the voice queries.

"Pepperoni and mushrooms," you answer.

"Address?" is the final question.

"1 Oak Street," you reply.

"Thirty minutes," you hear as the phone clicks off.

The steps you have just performed conform to the PizzaOrdering interface, which is implemented by thousands of pizza shops all over the world. You provide information on the size and toppings and where to deliver the desired pizza. The response is the amount of time until it will be delivered.

Using the same interface but with potentially different implementations is the central concept of *polymorphism*. Multiple pizza shops provide the same functionality. If I picked up the phone, dialed the number, and handed the phone to you, you might not know from which particular shop you were ordering. But you would use the same interaction with any pizza shop. In addition, you would not have any knowledge of how they really make the pizza. This interface does not constrain how the pizza shop makes its pizza, how many people they employ, the brand of flour they use, or anything else about the implementation.

How did you find an implementation of the PizzaOrdering interface? You probably used an implementation of the PizzaOrderingFinder interface. You looked in a directory under *Pizza*, went down the list of names, and picked one you used before or one that had been recommended to you by a friend. If you're in a new place, you may just start with the first name on the list. We'll explore other ways to find pizza shops later in this book.

PizzaOrderingFinder returns a pizza shop. Each pizza shop is different; otherwise, there would be no need for more than one brand of pizza shop. Shops vary on the quality of implementation: how fast they make the pizza and the tastefulness of the result. You may be aware of the variations between different pizza shops and ask PizzaOrderingFinder to find one whose characteristics fit your needs. If you're really hungry, you might substitute speed for quality. Pizza shops also vary on price (the requirements on the resources in your wallet). Whether resource requirements bear any relationship to quality is an interesting question that we'll discuss later in regard to software.

The Pizza Interfaces

Now for those readers who are having a hard time relating pizza to software development, let's create a more formal definition of the PizzaOrdering interface. We'll use this example later in the book as we describe the various facets of interfaces.

```
interface PizzaOrdering
    enumeration Size {SMALL, MEDIUM, LARGE}
```

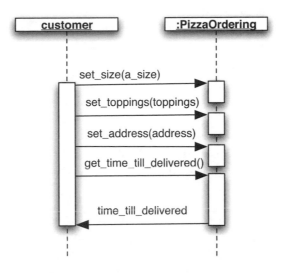

Figure 1.1: PizzaOrdering SEQUENCE DIAGRAM

```
enumeration Toppings {PEPPERONI, MUSHROOMS, PEPPERS, SAUSAGE}
set_size(Size)
set_toppings(Toppings [])
set_address(String street_address)
TimePeriod get_time_till_delivered()
```

Note that setting the address in our simulated conversation actually returned the time_till_delivered. Having a function that sets a value return a value of a completely different type gives me a bad feeling in my stomach, and it ain't from the pepperoni. So I added a method to retrieve the time_till_delivered.

Figure 1.1 shows the PizzaOrdering interface in a UML sequence diagram. The diagram captures the sequence of interaction between a customer and an implementation of the PizzaOrdering interface (i.e., a pizza shop). For those less familiar with sequence diagrams, I'll explain the details in Chapter 2.[1]

Here's a more formal description for how you might find a pizza shop:

---

[1]You may look at this interface and say, "I know another way to do this." Good! Write it down. If you don't see an equivalent interface later in this book, send it to me. I'll present several variations of interfaces in this book, but there is never one "best" answer, and alternatives are always worth considering.

```
interface PizzaOrderingFinder
    PizzaOrdering find_implementation_by_name
        (String name_of_pizza_shop);
    PizzaOrdering find_first_implementation()
    PizzaOrdering find_default_implementation()
```

This interface finds vendors that implement the PizzaOrdering interface. An implementation might not necessarily be a pizza shop; it might be a regular restaurant that offers pizzas as a menu item for delivery. It could be Sammy's Computer and Snack Shop that started offering pizzas when Sammy discovered that software development made programmers hungry.

You could realize this interface in a number of ways. You could perform the operations yourself by grabbing a phone book and getting a number and dialing it. You could ask a friend to do that for you. You could call the operator and ask for a particular pizza shop. This variation of possible implementations is another example of polymorphism in action. The PizzaOrderingFinder interface illustrates another pattern that will be discussed later in this book.[2]

1.2 Real-Life Interfaces

Software is not developed by pizza alone, even though it fuels much development. Let's first see what a software interface is all about, and then we'll explore examples of interfaces that exist in current systems.

What Is an Interface?

Interfaces are declared in code. In some languages, such as Java and C#, **interface** is a keyword. It applies to a set of method signatures (names and parameter lists). You use **implements** in Java to show that a class implements an interface. For example:

```
interface SampleInterface
    {
    double findAverage(double [] numbers);
    }
```

---

[2]In particular, the Factory Method pattern. See *Design Patterns: Elements of Reusable Object-Oriented Software* by Erich Gamma, Richard Helm, Ralph Johnson, and John Vlissides (Addison-Wesley, 1995).

```
class SampleImplementation implements SampleInterface
    {
    double findAverage(double [] numbers)
        {
        // calculate average and return it
        return average;
        }
    }
```

In C#, you define an interface with the **interface** keyword, but you use a colon (:) to show that an class implements the interface. Since the same symbol is used to show inheritance, by convention the interface name usually begins with *I*, as in the following example:

```
interface ISampleInterface
    {
    double findAverage(double [] numbers);
    }
class SampleImplementation : ISampleInterface
    {
    double findAverage(double [] numbers)
        {
        // calculate average and return it
        return average;
        }
    }
```

C++ programmers do not have an equivalent keyword; in C++ a class with all pure virtual functions (described by using " =0" for the function body) and with no data members is the code equivalent of an interface.[3] You use the inheritance symbol (:), even though there is no implementation to inherit.

```
class SampleInterface
    {
    double findAverage(double numbers [], int size) = 0;
    }
class SampleImplementation : public SampleInterface
    {
    double findAverage(int numbers [], int size)
        {
        // calculate average and return it
        return average;
        }
    };
```

---

[3]An interface can have enumeration definitions.

Other Interfaces

Even a non-object-oriented language, such as C, can support interfaces. In C, an interface is a set of functions that apply to a common concept, such as the set of functions that operate on a file, as we'll explore in the next section.[4]

Text is another form of interface. The text specifies the functions to perform (typically in a human-readable format but not necessarily). For example, the command prompt of Windows is a textual interface—you type a command to perform along with parameters. We will use the term *textual interface* to differentiate this type of interface from one in a programming language.

Unix Devices

The Unix operating system has a standard interface to all devices (hard drives, displays, printers, and keyboards) and files, and it is expressed in the C language. This interface is an example of polymorphism in a non-object-oriented language: you always use the same functions, regardless of the type of device or file.

To the user, each device appears as a file. Every device has an entry in the file system in the /dev directory. For example, a printer entry might be /dev/lp0 (for line printer 0). You open and write to a printer in the same way you write to a file. The basic set of functions include the following:[5]

```
open(filename, flags);
    // Returns a file descriptor.
    // Flags include O_RDONLY, O_WRONLY or O_RDWR
close(file_descriptor);
read(file_descriptor, buffer, count);
write(file_descriptor, buffer, count);
```

For example, you open a file with this:

```
file_descriptor1 = open("/home/ken/myfile.txt", O_WRONLY);
```

To open a printer, you use:

```
file_descriptor2 = open("/dev/lp0", O_WRONLY);
```

---

[4]In C, a structure that contains members that are function pointers acts as a polymorphic interface. For example, the file_operations structure for device drivers in Linux describes the functions that a driver must support.

[5]This is a simplified version.

After this point, the remainder of your program reads and writes using the file descriptors. The calls to these functions are the same, regardless of whether you are communicating to a file or the printer. For example, both of these function calls write nine characters to the corresponding device:

```
write(file_descriptor1, "Something", 9);
write(file_descriptor2, "Something", 9);
```

The polymorphism that this interface provides is powerful. Suppose you write a program that is intended to read from the keyboard and write to the display. You can freely substitute other devices for the keyboard and the display. From the command line, this is known as I/O redirection. Because there is no difference between reading from a file and reading from the keyboard, you can put commands into a file and have a program read the commands from that file.[6]

For example, the cat program (short for *concatenate*) is nominally set so that input comes from the keyboard and output goes to a display. Using I/O redirection, if you write

```
cat < input_file > output_file
```

cat reads from input_file and writes to output_file. Suppose you want to display your entire hard disk, assuming you have the necessary privilege to read the device. You can use the following:

```
cat < /dev/hda1
```

You can copy an entire disk to another disk as simply as doing this:

```
cat < /dev/hda1 > /dev/hda2
```

The Interface

Object diehards might not consider the preceding set of C functions to be an interface. The set of functions follows a common pattern that starts with initiating a service request (open()) that returns an opaque data identifier (a file descriptor). The identifier is passed to other functions (write(), read(), and close()) for subsequent processing. Service patterns like this can be transformed into a more familiar-looking interface. A realization of this interface will have a file descriptor as a private data member, but that is an implementation detail that is not part of an interface.

---

[6]You can also use the polymorphic behavior to set the output of one program to be the input of another program. Unix systems refer to this as a *pipe*.

```
interface File
    open(filename, flags) signals UnableToOpen
    read(buffer, count) signals EndOfFile, UnableToRead
    write(buffer, count) signals UnableToWrite,
    close()
```

We'll look at this interface again in a few chapters, so if this thin veneer doesn't particularly appeal to you at the moment, wait a while, and we'll fix it up.

Textual Interfaces

Since every device in Unix operates through a common interface, you need some method to communicate device-specific commands. One way is to use a textual interface for these directives. The commands are sent as a string of characters. A common textual interface is the original modem interface created by the manufacturer Hayes. For example, some of the common commands are as follows:

AT (attention, commands follow)

D (dial a number)

T (dial a number using tones, rather than pulses)

To dial a number, you send the modem the "ATDT9195551212" sequence. The replies from the modem are also textual. If the connection was successful, the modem returns the "CONNECT" string. If the connection was not successful, it returns a string denoting the error, as the "NO CARRIER" or "BUSY" string. To hang up the phone, you send the "ATH" string.

An advantage of a textual interface is that you can store the commands in a file. Later you can read the file and send them to the device.

Other textual interfaces include the common Internet protocols such as Simple Mail Transfer Protocol (SMTP) and File Transfer Protocol (FTP). For example, FTP commands include the following:

```
open hostname     #Open a connection
get filename      #Get a file
close             #Close a connection
```

You may run across other textual interfaces, although you might not necessarily think of them as such. Both Unix and Windows can create text files containing commands and data for printers; a standard language for these commands is PostScript. The document is text, so it can be stored in a file or sent to a printer device. An example of PostScript commands to print "Hello world" on a page is as follows:

```
/Times-Roman findfont
12 scalefont
setfont
newpath
200 300 moveto
(Hello world) show
showpage
```

The printer interprets the commands and prints the page. The set of printers that understand PostScript can be considered polymorphic implementations of the PostScript interface.[7] Just like pizza shops, their output may vary in quality and speed. But they all implement the same functionality.

We'll examine in Chapter 3 how to translate a textual interface, such as the FTP commands, into a programmatic interface. The PostScript file acts like a document-style interface. We'll explore document-style interfaces in more detail in Chapter 6.

The GUI Interface

Packages that support graphical user interfaces make extensive use of polymorphism. In both Java and Windows, you draw in a graphics context. In Java, the context is the Graphics class. For Windows, the graphic context for the Microsoft Foundation Classes (MFC) is the CDC (for *device context*) class. The graphics context could refer to a display, a printer, an in-memory screen buffer, or a metafile. The user drawing on the graphics context may not be aware to what they are actually outputting.

In Java, you call drawString() to output a string to the display at a particular position:

```
void drawString(String string, int x, int y);
```

Given a reference to a Graphics object (say g), to output the string you would code this:

```
g.drawString("Hello world", 200, 300);
```

For example, in MFC, you write text to the device context using the following method:

---

[7]You can display PostScript files on Windows and Unix with GSView (http://www.cs.wisc.edu/~ghost/gsview/get47.htm).

```
BOOL TextOut(int x, int y, const CString & string);
```

With a pointer to a CDC object (say, pDC), the code to output a string is as follows:[8]

```
pDC->TextOut(200, 300, "Hello world");
```

Both graphics contexts are state-based interfaces; they contain the current font with which the text is drawn as well as a plethora of other items. In Chapter 3, we'll see how we can translate this state-based interface to a non-state-based interface.

The PostScript text in the previous section and these two code examples perform the same operation. All three represent a realization of an interface that you could declare as follows:

```
interface DisplayOutput
    write_text(x_position, y_position, text)
```

I'll describe many of the interfaces in this book at this level of detail. This is to emphasize the functionality that an interface provides, rather than the detailed code for any particular language.

1.3 Things to Remember

We've begun our exploration of interfaces with an emphasis on polymorphism. You've seen interfaces with a variety of functionality—from ordering pizza to writing to devices to displaying text. You've seen the same functionality as expressed in a programmatic interface and a textual interface. In the next chapter we'll get down to business and discuss contracts that modules make when they implement an interface.

---

[8]The values of 200 and 300 in these examples do not refer to the same coordinate system. For PostScript, the values are in points (1/72"). For drawstring(), the values are in pixels.

Chapter 2

Interface Contracts

In this chapter, we're going to examine contracts. These contracts are not the ones you make when you order pizzas but are the contracts between the users of interfaces and their implementation. If you or the implementation violates the contract, you will not get what you want, so understanding contracts is essential.

We'll start by considering three laws that all implementations should obey, regardless of what services they offer. Then we'll look at Bertrand Meyer's *Design by Contract* that outlines conditions for methods. You cannot be sure that an implementation fulfills its contract until you test it; contracts for pizzas and for files offer an opportunity to show types of tests you can apply to interfaces. Also, you don't measure the quality of a pizza by just its speed of delivery. The nonfunctional qualities of pizza are also important, so we conclude with a look at implementation quality.

2.1 The Three Laws of Interfaces

One way to express one of the facets of the contract for an interface is with three principles inspired by the Three Laws of Robotics. Isaac Asimov first presented these laws in 1950 in his short-story collection, *Robot*.[1] Since computer programs often act like robots, this analogy of the laws seems appropriate.

---

[1]You can find the original laws, as well as more details, at http://www.asimovonline.com/.

1. An Interface's Implementation Shall Do What Its Methods Says It Does

This law may seem fairly obvious. The name of a method should correspond to the operations that the implementation actually performs.[2]

Conversely, an implementation should perform the operations intended by the creator of the interface. The method should return a value or signal an error in accordance with the explained purpose of the method.

If the purpose and meaning of a method are not unambiguously obvious from the method's name and its place within an interface, then those aspects should be clearly documented.[3] The documentation may refer to interface tests, such as those described later in this chapter, to demonstrate method meaning in a practical, usage context.

An implementation needs to honor the meaning of a return value. The sample PizzaOrdering interface in the previous chapter included the method TimePeriod get_time_till_delivered(). The return value represents the amount of time until the pizza shows up on your doorstep. A delivery should take no more than this amount of time. If TimePeriod is reported in whole minutes, an implementation that rounds down an internal calculated time (e.g., 5.5 minutes to 5 minutes) will return a value that does not correspond to the described meaning.

2. An Interface Implementation Shall Do No Harm

Harm refers to an implementation interfering with other modules in a program or with other programs. The user of an interface implementation should expect that the implementation performs its services in an efficient manner.[4]

In particular, an implementation should not hog resources. Resources in this case might include time, memory, file handles, database connections, and threads. For example, if the implementation requires connecting to a database that has limited connections, it should disconnect as soon as the required database operation is complete. Alter-

---

[2]This is also known as the *Principle of Least Surprises*.

[3]Michael Hunter suggests, "They should be documented regardless. Conversely, if they need documentation, the name should be improved."

[4]Andy Hunt suggests that implementation should use only those resources suggested by its interface. For example, an interface whose purpose is to write to the screen should not require a database connection.

Liskov Substitution Principle

The first law corresponds to the Liskov Substitution Principle (LSP), which states that a subtype should be indistinguishable in behavior from the type from which it is derived. For object design, methods in a base class should be applicable to derived classes. In another words, a derived class should obey the contract of the base class. Thus, any object of a derived class is "substitutable" as an object of the base class. Barbara Liskov and Jennette Wing introduced this principle in their paper "Family Values: A Behavioral Notion of Subtyping."*

---

*The full discussion is at `http://www.lcs.mit.edu/publications/pubs/pdf/MIT-LCS-TR-562b.pdf`.

---

natively, the implementation could use a shared connection and release that connection as soon as the operation finishes.[5]

If an implementation uses excessive memory, then it may cause page faults that can slow down not only the program itself but also other programs.

3. If An Implementation Is Unable to Perform Its Responsibilities, It Shall Notify Its Caller

An implementation should always report problems that are encountered and that it cannot fix itself. The manner of report (e.g., the error signal) can either be a return code or be an exception. For example, if the implementation requires a connection to a web service (as described in Chapter 5) and it cannot establish that connection, then it should report the problem. If there are two or more providers of a web service, then the implementation should try to establish a connection with each of the providers.

---

[5]For example, implementations of J2EE Enterprise JavaBeans (EJBs) interfaces share connections.

> ### ༄ Joe Asks. . .
> #### What's a Page Fault?
>
> If you've ever seen your computer pause and the disk light come on when you switch between two programs, you've seen the effects of page faults. Here's what happens.
>
> A computer has a limited amount of memory. Memory is divided into pages, typically 16 KB each. If a number of programs are running simultaneously, the total number of pages they require may exceed the amount of physical memory. The operating system uses the disk drive to store the contents of pages that cannot fit in physical memory and that programs are not currently accessing. The disk drive acts as "virtual" memory.
>
> When a program accesses a page not in physical memory (a page fault), the operating system writes the current contents of a memory page to disk and retrieves the accessed page from the drive. The more memory required by programs, the greater the chance that virtual memory is required and thus the greater possibility of page faults and the slower the program will run.

Only if it is unable to connect to any of them should it report the problem to the caller.[6,7]

The errors that are denoted on the interface (either return codes or exceptions) are part of the interface contract; an interface should produce *only* those errors. An implementation should handle nonspecified situations gracefully. It should report an error if it cannot determine a reasonable course of action.

---

[6]Michael Hunter notes that there can be hidden dangers if each interface implementation implements a retry process. An implementation may call another interface implementation. If both of them perform retries, then the report of failure to the user will take longer. In one application, this failure report took more than five minutes because of the number of interfaces in the process.

[7]For debugging or other purposes, the implementation may log the unsuccessful attempts to connect with each of the services.

Reporting Errors

You call the pizza shop.

You start to place the order, "I'd like a large pizza."

The voice comes back, "Johnny isn't here."

You say, "With pepperoni," not having really listened to the previous statement.

The voice says, "Johnny isn't here."

"So?" you say.

The voice says, "So, we can't make a pizza."

You hang up.

It turns out Johnny is the cook. He's not there. What do you care? You really can't do anything about that implementation detail. The voice should say at the beginning, "I'm sorry, but we can't make any pizza today." You really do not care why. You cannot call Johnny and tell him to go to work.

An interface should report problems only in terms that are meaningful to the user. What are the potential problems for the pizza shop?

- *Unable to make pizza:* As a customer, your response is to hang up and find another pizza shop.

- *Unable to deliver pizza:* You could decide to pick up the pizza, or you could try another pizza shop.

Technology exceptions should be converted into business exceptions. Suppose the method returns a technology exception such as RemoteException. Then the interface is tied to a particular implementation. Instead, the method should return a business exception, such as UnableToObtainIngredients. If more detailed information is required for debugging purposes, it can be placed as data within the business exception.

2.2 Design by Contract

To successfully use an interface, both the caller and implementer need to understand the contract—what the implementation agrees to do for the caller. You can start with informal documentation of that agreement. Then, if necessary, you can create a standard contract.

Bertrand Meyer popularized Design by Contract in his book *Object-Oriented Software Construction* (Prentice Hall, 1997). In the book, he discusses standards for contracts between a method and a caller.[8] He introduces three facets to a contract—preconditions, postconditions, and class invariants.

The user of an interface needs to ensure that certain conditions are met when calling a method; these stipulations are the *preconditions*. Each method in an interface specifies certain conditions that will be true after its invocation is complete; those guarantees are the *postconditions*. The third aspect is the *class invariant,* which describes the conditions that every object instance must satisfy. When dealing with interfaces, these class invariants are typically properties of a particular implementation, not of the interface methods.

If a precondition is not met, the method may operate improperly. If the preconditions are met and a postcondition is not met, the method has not worked properly.[9] Any implementation of an interface can have weaker preconditions and stronger postconditions. This follows the concept that a derived class can have weaker preconditions and stronger postconditions than the base class.

Contract Checking

An interface implementation is not required to check the preconditions. You may assume that the user has met those preconditions. If the user has not, the implementation is free to fail. Any failures should be reported as in the Third Law of Interfaces.

If you decide to check the preconditions, you can do so in a number of ways:

---

[8]See http://archive.eiffel.com/doc/manuals/technology/contract/ for a discussion of contracts for components.

[9]You can use the Object Constraint Language (OCL) in UML to document the preconditions and postconditions.

Pizza Conditions

Suppose a pizza-ordering interface specified that the allowed toppings are pepperoni, mushrooms, and pineapple. An implementation that provides only pepperoni and mushrooms would work only for a limited range of pizzas. It has stronger preconditions. A pizza shop that also offered broccoli and ham has weaker preconditions. An implementation with weaker preconditions can meet the contract for the interface. One that has stronger preconditions cannot.

Likewise, suppose that your requirement for delivery time is a half hour. A pizza shop that may take up to one hour has a weaker postcondition. One that may deliver in ten minutes has a stronger postcondition. An implementation with stronger postconditions meets the contract; one with weaker postconditions does not.

- You could use code embedded within each method to check the conditions.

- In a less imposing way, you could use aspects,[10] if a particular language supports them.

- A third way is to use a contract-checking proxy. Chapter 11 describes the Proxy pattern.[11]

- nContracts is a C# language specific method. nContracts uses C# attributes to specify the preconditions and postconditions. It does not require change to the implementation source (like aspects), but works like a contract checking proxy.[12]

A contract-checking proxy is an implementation of the interface that checks the preconditions for each method. If all preconditions are met, the proxy calls the corresponding method in the implementation that does the actual work. Otherwise, it signals failure. If the corresponding method returns and the postconditions are not met, it could also signal failure.

---

[10]See aspect-oriented programming at http://aosd.net/

[11]The pattern can also be considered the Decorator pattern. See also *Design Patterns*.

[12]See http://puzzleware.net/nContract/nContract.html.

Pizza Contract

Let's take a look at the PizzaOrdering interface. What are the contractual obligations of this interface? OK, the pizza shop agrees to make and deliver a pizza, and you also have to pay for the pizza. But you have other facets. The interface requires a certain flow to be followed. If you started by saying "1 Oak Street," the order taker may get really flustered and try to make you an Oak-sized pizza. So, the conditions for each of the methods are as follows:

Method	Preconditions	Postconditions
set_size()	None	Size set
set_toppings()	Size has been set	Toppings set
set_address	Size and toppings set	Address set
get_time_till_delivered	Size, toppings, address set	None

Now you may want an interface that is a little less restrictive. You might think you ought to be able to set the size, toppings, and address in any order. You would eliminate the preconditions for the three set methods, but the one for get_time_till_delivered() would still remain. For a product as simple as a pizza, the strictness of the order is probably unwarranted. For a more complex product, the method order may be essential. For example, if you're ordering a car, you can't choose the options until you've chosen the model.

File Contract

For a more computer-related example, let's examine the contract for the File interface we introduced in Chapter 1. Here's the interface again:

```
interface File
    open(filename, flags) signals UnableToOpen
    read(buffer,count) signals EndOfFile, UnableToRead
    write(buffer, count) signals UnableToWrite
    close()
```

Before we investigate the contract for this interface, let's examine the abstraction that this interface represents. A realization of this interface has these responsibilities:

Method	Preconditions	Postconditions

open(filename, flags) signals UnableToOpen	None	If (for writing)
		 if user has permission
		  File is opened for writing
		
		if (for reading)
		 if file exists and
		  user has permission
		   File is opened for reading

read(buffer, count) signals EndOfFile, UnableToRead	File opened for reading	If not at end of file If count < bytes left in file Set file position to bytes after current else Set file position to end of file
write(buffer, count) signals UnableToWrite	File opened for writing	File position incremented by count
close()	File is open	File closed

Figure 2.1: PRE- AND POSTCONDITIONS FOR FILE INTERFACE

For writing out

> Output a sequence of bytes to the device or file in the order in which they are sent.

For reading from

> Input a sequence of bytes from the device or file in the order in which they are received or read.

For files (not devices)

> Save the output sequence of bytes for later retrieval by another process. The saved sequence should persist after a system shutdown and reboot.

The contract for this interface includes the preconditions and postconditions shown in Figure 2.1.

If the caller does not call open(), the other methods will fail. They should inform the caller of the failure. They should not cause harm in the event of this failure (see the Second Law of Interfaces). For example, suppose an implementation initialized a reference in open(). Without calling open(), that reference is uninitialized (e.g., null). If the write method attempted to use that uninitialized reference and an exception or memory fault resulted, that would violate the second law.

Protocol

You can list the operations involved in an interface, including preconditions, postconditions, parameters and their types, return values, and errors signaled. But you need more than just how to use operations and when to use each operation. You also need to know the protocol to the interface—the set of allowable sequences of method calls. The preconditions often imply a sequence, but they may not. The protocol can also show the callbacks that an interface may create, events that are generated, or observers that are called.

For the File interface, you must follow a distinct sequence of methods. You must open a file before you can read, write, or close it. The protocol can be documented in words, in a sequence diagram, in a state diagram, or in test code.

To express the protocol in words, I use a form of a use case.[13] A use case describes an interaction between a user and a system that fulfills a goal. An internal use case describes an interaction between a caller and an interface. To differentiate between the two cases, I refer to an internal use case as a *work case*. Use cases are usually expressed in technology-independent terms; work cases might include the names of the methods in the interface. The work cases demonstrate the protocol for an interface.

For the File interface, we have the following work cases:

 Work Case: Read a File

1. Open a file for reading (open()).

2. Read bytes from file (read()).

3. Close file (close()).

---

[13]For more details, see *Writing Effective Use Cases* by Alistair Cockburn (Addison-Wesley, 2000) and http://alistair.cockburn.us/crystal/articles/sucwg/structuringucswithgoals.htm.

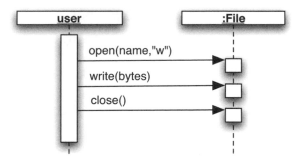

Figure 2.2: SEQUENCE DIAGRAM FOR THE PROTOCOL

Work Case: Write a File

1. Open a file for writing (open()).

2. Write bytes to file (write()).

3. Close file (close()).

A UML sequence diagram can also demonstrate the protocol. Figure 2.2 shows the sequence diagram that corresponds to the second work case.

A UML state diagram provides a different way of indicating a protocol. For each state, it shows what methods you can call. Calls to methods may alter the state of an implementation and therefore alter what other methods you may call.

For a file, the states include CLOSED, and OPEN_FOR_READING, OPEN_FOR_WRITING. If an error, such as reading a file opened for writing, causes the file to become unusable, you could have an ERROR state.[14]

Figure 2.3, on the next page shows the state diagram for File. Note that read() and write() transition into the ERROR state, if the file has been opened in the opposite mode. The diagram does not show transitions

---

[14]Note in many languages, there are input streams and output streams. You cannot invoke read on an output stream or write on an input stream, since the methods do not exist in the corresponding interfaces. That separation of interfaces decreases the number of possible state transitions and possible ways that errors can be generated.

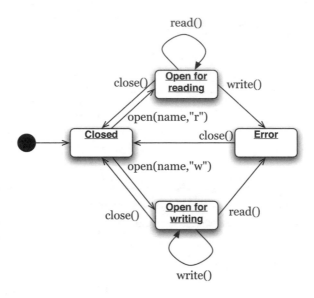

Figure 2.3: STATE DIAGRAM FOR FILE

from ERROR for read() and write(). So, these method calls are ignored in that state, according to the diagram.[15]

2.3 Testing Interfaces against Contracts

There is no question that automated unit and acceptance testing dramatically help in developing software. Extreme Programming (XP) and other agile processes have reemphasized and reinvigorated the concepts of testing. But what are you testing for? Essentially, you are testing to ensure that an implementation of an interface meets its contract. You can specify a contract in documentation; however, a coded test can make the contractual obligation clearer. Plus, it can verify that the contract is met. As a general rule, no interface definition is complete until you have all the contractual tests successfully running for at least one implementation.

---

[15]We leave it up to you to determine for your particular language or operating system whether there is an implied ERROR state and what happens with an incorrect use of read() and write(). See whether the documentation clearly describes the situation.

/\\/ **Joe Asks...**

What's a UML Sequence Diagram?

A UML sequence diagram shows a sequence of interactions between modules. The interactions take the form of messages or method calls. The modules may be instances of classes or implementations of interfaces. A box and dotted line represent a module. The name is within the box. The name may represent an actual module or an unspecified implementation of an interface. To show the latter, you use a colon before the name of the interface. The dotted line represents the "life" of the module. For example, for an object, the line represents how long the object exists.

You show calls to a method by drawing a line between the caller and the callee and giving the name of the method. Lines in the reverse direction show return values from methods.

When an implementation is "active" (that is, doing something rather than just existing), the lifeline shows up as a rectangle, rather than a dotted line.*

*This explanation gives only facets of sequence diagrams that we use in this book. More details are at http://www.sparxsystems.com/resources/uml2_tutorial/.

The *Design Patterns* book states, "Design to an interface, not an implementation." A parallel guideline exists in testing. "Test to an interface, not an implementation". This is termed *black box* testing.[16] You test an interface without looking inside to see how it is coded. With more services being provided remotely, you probably will not have access to the code. Therefore, you can test only to the interface.

Writing tests for an interface can also help you work out difficulties in the interface. You can find ambiguities or unclearness in the contractual obligations, the method definitions, or the protocol. If you find that your interface is hard to test, then it probably will be hard to use. If this happens, you can redesign your interface without even having coded an implementation.

---

[16]*White box* testing uses knowledge of the code to devise tests, typically tests that check performance and robustness.

Joe Asks...

What's a State Diagram?

A state diagram shows states and how method calls (or other events) cause transitions between states. The diagram has an initial state marked by a line from a filled circle. A rounded rectangle represents each state. Lines with method names represent the transitions between states. A circle with a dot in it marks the termination of the state transition.

Showing transitions for all methods for each state can complicate a diagram. Accompanying text can explain whether methods not shown on a transition line are ignored or cause an implicit transition that terminates the state diagram.*

---

*This explanation gives facets only of state diagrams that we use in this book. More details are at `http://www.sparxsystems.com/resources/uml2_tutorial/`.

Tests for the Pizza Contract

Let's devise tests for the PizzaOrdering interface. We can create tests for each individual method. But we also want to create a test for a work case, which calls all the corresponding methods.[17] This is the test for the work case:

 Test Case: Order a Pizza

1. Set the size (set_size()).

2. Set the toppings (set_toppings()).

3. Set the address (set_address()).

4. Call get_time_till_delivered().

5. Verify that a pizza is delivered to the address within the returned time_till_delivered.

---

[17]Note that testing an implementation to ensure it is successful for all the combinations of sizes and toppings could be expensive, time-consuming, and fattening. See Elisabeth Hendrickson's article (`http://www.qualitytree.com/ruminate/022105.htm`) for how to devise tests for random combinations.

Tests for the File Contract

For the File interface, we devise tests for each of the work cases, as well as for the individual methods. The tests for the two work cases would include the following:[18]

Test Case: Write Bytes to File

1. Open a file for writing.

2. Write a number of bytes that have known values.

3. Close file.

4. Verify that the bytes have been written.

Test Case: Read Bytes from File

1. Open a file for reading.

2. Read a number of bytes.

3. Verify that the bytes are equal to known values.

4. Close file.

We can create "*misuse*" cases (or "*miswork*" cases). Misuse cases state ways that a caller or user might accidentally (or deliberately) violate the protocol. Here are some misuse cases for File:

Test Case: Read a File Opened for Writing

1. Open a file for writing.

2. Read bytes from file. This operation should signal an error.

3. Close file.

Test Case: Write to an Unopened File

1. Write bytes to file. This operation should signal an error.

You should ensure that you have tests for all possible sequences of method calls. A state diagram such as Figure 2.3, on page 24, can clarify the sequences that need testing. For example, in addition to the

---

[18]These tests represent only a portion of the tests. We would also create variations that include writing zero bytes, a single byte, and a large number of bytes.

previous tests, we should try writing to a file opened for writing and then reading from it.

2.4 Levels of Contracts

Christine Mingins and Jean-Marc Jézéquel suggest that there are several levels of contracts.[19] The levels are:

- Basic type contracts as in typed programming languages

- Semantic contracts that include the preconditions and postconditions

- Performance contracts for real-time systems

- Quality of service contracts that are hard to quantify

You need to test for conformance with all these contracts. For typed programming languages, the compiler enforces the type contract (we'll take a look at untyped languages in the next section). Testing for quality of service contracts is usually more difficult than testing for performance contracts: quality may include resource usage, reliability, scalability, and the other "ilities."[20] We'll examine quality more shortly.

Other nonfunctional facets of interfaces include transactional behavior (does it participate in a transaction?), security (e.g., is it called by or on behalf of authorized users?), and logging. These facets can be applied by aspect-based code, such as Java aspects, or by frameworks, such as J2EE, in which the implementations reside. In either case, the interface implementation has code only for the essential behavior. The aspects or framework take care of the rest. We don't cover security or transactions in this book, because they require entire books by themselves.

Explicit versus Implicit Type Contracts

Languages differ in how they enforce the parameter data type contracts. In some languages, such as Java and C++, you have to be explicit about the data types of the parameters that are passed to a method. In other languages, such as Python, Perl, and Ruby, the data type is implicit.

---

[19]See http://archive.eiffel.com/doc/manuals/technology/bmarticles/sd/contracts.html.

[20]See *Software Requirements* by Karl Wiegers (Microsoft Press, 2003) for a full discussion of the "ilities."

You do not specify a parameter type. How a method uses a parameter implies the type.

Let's look at an example of implicit typing in the Observer pattern.[21] In this common pattern, one object is interested in changes in the state of another object. The interested party is the observer, and the watched party is the observed.

Suppose we have a Customer class. An observer may be interested in the event that the name or the address changed in the class. If we program this class in an dynamically typed language such as Ruby, we might code this:[22]

```
class Customer
    def add_observer(observer)
        @observer = observer
    end

    def address=(new_address)
        @address=new_address
        @observer.notify_address_change(new address)
    end

    def name=(new_name)
        @name=new_name
        @observer.notify_name_change(new_name)
    end
```

Note that observer must have two methods. If set_address() or set_name() is called and the observer does not have a matching notify() method, a runtime error occurs. The error occurs because the implicit contract (having these two methods) has been violated.

In Java, the methods required by an observer are described by an explicit interface:[23]

```
interface CustomerObserver
    notify_address_change(address)
    notify_name_change(name)
```

You state explicitly that the observer must have these methods by its type declaration in the parameter list for add_observer(). For example:

---

[21]See *Design Patterns* for more details on the Observer pattern.

[22]In Ruby, we could also use the Observer mixin.

[23]This has been reduced from the usual multiple observers to a single observer to keep the code simple.

```
class Customer
    {
    CustomerObserver the_observer;
    void add_observer(CustomerObserver observer)
        {
        the_observer = observer;
        }
    void set_address(Address an_address)
        {
        // set address, then
        observer.notify_address_change(an_address)
        }
    void set_name(name)
        {
        // set name, then
        observer.notify_name_change(name)
        }
    }
```

The Java compiler complains if you pass an object that does not provide the CustomerObserver interface to the add_observer() method.

In both Ruby and Java, you should write sufficient tests to ensure that the observer/observed code works as you intended. So, one might argue that an explicit interface is not required. However, typing the parameter as CustomerObserver enforces in code the contract that the object must support those methods. With implicit typing, the need for the methods must be shown in the documentation.

2.5 Contractual Quality

We introduced a question in the original pizza example of whether price has any relationship to quality; we might also ask whether speed of delivery is more important than tastiness. We're going to let these questions of pizza be an area of discussion for you and your fellow readers of this book.

But these questions do have important analogies in software—the quality of implementation trade-offs. For example, one implementation of an interface might be faster but require more memory.

The speed of an implementation can vary based on the demands placed upon it. This makes it tricky if you cannot determine in advance the requirements for the caller. For example, suppose you had a method sort(Object ()) that sorted the passed array using a comparison function of Object class.[24] There are many different algorithms for sorting an array. They differ in speed and memory resources required.[25] The algorithms' variance in speed is often due to the degree of sorting already in the array. For example, if an array is already sorted, a bubble sort is the fastest, but the quicksort algorithm is faster than a bubble sort most of the time. If the array is already sorted in the reverse direction, quicksort is slower by far. Because of its recursive nature, quicksort can demand somewhat more resources than the bubble sort. By using interfaces to a sorting method, rather than specifying a particular one, you can always substitute an implementation that is more aligned with the requirements that spontaneously arise.

The sort example is a specific case of the general issue that implementation trade-offs are important. By using interfaces, rather than concrete implementations, you can make choices appropriate to a given situation without having to alter code that uses the interface.

2.6 Things to Remember

An implementation of an interface should obey the three laws:

- Do what its methods say it does.

- Do no harm.

- Notify its caller with meaningful errors if unable to perform its responsibilities.

Establish a contract for each interface (either formally or informally):

- Indicate the preconditions and postconditions for each method.

- Specify the protocol—the sequence of allowable method calls.

- Optionally, spell out nonfunctional aspects such as performance or quality of implementation.

- Create tests to check that an implementation performs according to its contract and that it obeys the three laws.

---

[24]You might supply a comparison function to the method to make the sort more flexible.

[25]Donald E. Knuth's classic book on sorting and searching gives a whole slew of algorithms: *Art of Computer Programming, Volume 3: Sorting and Searching* (Addison-Wesley, 1998).

Sudoku and Quality

You may have noticed in your newspaper a new puzzle that has nine columns and rows and some digits in the boxes. The digits are a clue to the name Sudoku. Sudoku is an abbreviation for a phrase meaning "the digits must remain single." To complete the puzzle, you fill in the empty boxes with the digits 1 to 9. Every row and every column must contain every digit (i.e., without repetition, since there are nine digits and nine boxes). In addition, there are nine sets of three-by-three boxes that must also contain every digit once.*

At this point, you're probably wondering what Sudoku has to do with interfaces. Stay with me a moment....

When I saw the puzzle for the first time, I immediately thought of how I could program the solution. It turns out I was not alone. David Bock, who reviewed this book, also programmed a solution. He created a program that allows him to test the relative quality of implementations of various solvers. The test program is invoked with this:

```
measure_sudoku puzzle_file java_solution_class_name
```

The puzzle_file contains one or more Sudoku puzzles. The java_solution_class_name is the name of a class (in the JAVA_PATH) that implements the Solver interface, which looks like this:

```
public interface Solver
    {
    public Board solve(Board inBoard);
    }
```

The `measure_sudoku` program reads the puzzle_file and turns each puzzle into a Board. It then calls solve() for each Board and records the amount of time the solution takes (you are welcome to test your own Sudoku solver by downloading this program from this book's web site). Often you only have the resources to create tests for the functional part of an interface contract. For instance, the original test program measured only the speed of solution. However, you should determine what nonfunctional aspects should also be tested and how to test for them. For a Solver, these aspects can include resource utilization, robustness, and completeness. Resource utilization can be measured by memory usage. For robustness, an unsolvable puzzle can be given to the solver. For completeness, a puzzle with multiple solutions can be passed to see whether a solver can find all the solutions.

*See http://www.sudoku.com for a manual solution.

Chapter 3

Interface Ingredients

Now that we've covered the basics of interfaces, it's time to examine the ingredients of interfaces. Almost every interface you employ or develop has a combination of these ingredients, so understanding them helps you appreciate the whole pie. In this chapter, we'll look at the spectrum of interfaces from data-oriented to service-oriented and cover the trade-offs in three distinct approaches to data-access interfaces.

You can always adapt an interface paradigm from one type to another to make it more amenable to your project, so we'll explore how to adapt a stateful interface to a stateless one. Then we'll look at transforming a textual interface into a programmatic one and creating an interface from a set of existing related methods.

3.1 Data Interfaces and Service Interfaces

There is a spectrum between data interfaces and service interfaces. We use the term *data interface* when the methods correspond to those in a class that contains mostly attributes. The methods in the interface typically set or retrieve the values of the attributes.[1] We use the term *service interface* for a module whose methods operate mostly on the parameters that are passed to it.

One example of a data interface is the classic Customer class. Customer usually has methods like

- set_name(String name)

---

[1]Data interfaces also correspond to JavaBeans or pretty much any class that is a wrapper around attributes with a bunch of getter/setters.

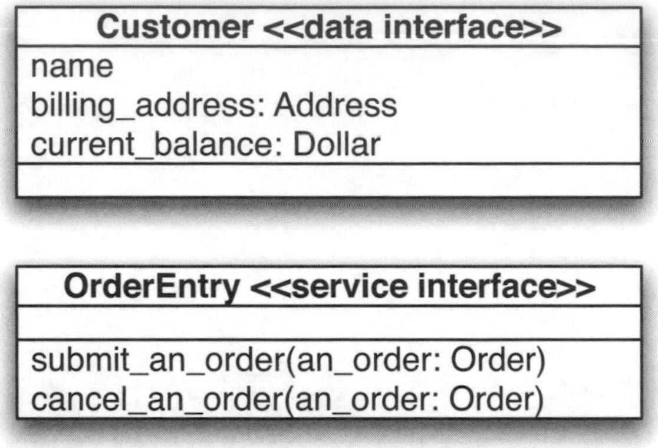

```
┌────────────────────────────────────┐
│      Customer <<data interface>>    │
├────────────────────────────────────┤
│ name                               │
│ billing_address: Address           │
│ current_balance: Dollar            │
├────────────────────────────────────┤
│                                    │
└────────────────────────────────────┘
```

```
┌────────────────────────────────────┐
│    OrderEntry <<service interface>> │
├────────────────────────────────────┤
│                                    │
├────────────────────────────────────┤
│ submit_an_order(an_order: Order)   │
│ cancel_an_order(an_order: Order)   │
└────────────────────────────────────┘
```

Figure 3.1: Data vs. service interface

- set_billing_address(Address billing_address)

- get_current_balance( ).

Each of these methods affects or uses an attribute in the class. Implementations of data interfaces have state, which consists of the set of values of all attributes in the class.

Service interfaces have methods that act on the parameters passed to them, rather than the attributes of the implementation, for example the methods submit_an_order(Order an_order) and cancel_an_order(Order an_order). Figure 3.1 shows how data interfaces have just attributes and service interfaces have just methods.

Service interface implementations usually have no attributes or only ones that are associated with providing the service, such as connection information that identifies where to submit an order or where to find the current price for a stock. Implementations of service interfaces may have no state, other than that of internal configuration values such as this connection information.

This data versus service interface comparison is not pure black and white, but rather a spectrum. An interface can range from a data transfer object (DTO), whose methods refer only to attributes of the object, to a command interface, which usually contains only service methods. We could move away from a pure data interface by adding methods to the Customer interface. We might add charge_an_amount(), which

Entities, Control, Boundary

In *Object-Oriented Software Engineering*, Ivar Jacobsen introduced three stereotypes for objects: entity, boundary, and control. An *entity* depicts long-lived objects. *Boundary* objects communicate between the system and the actors (users and external systems). A *control* object represents behavior related to a specific use case. It communicates with boundary objects and entity objects to perform an operation.

These stereotypes relate to the data and service interfaces. Data interfaces correspond to the entity objects. The underlying data mechanism (e.g., database table or XML file) is opaque to the user of the entity object. An interface such as Pizza, which contains just the size and toppings, is an entity.

A boundary corresponds to a service interface. You push a button on a GUI or make a call to a method, and the underlying service is performed. The PizzaOrdering interface presented in Chapter 1 is a boundary interface.

A controller also corresponds to a service interface. Its methods are typically called by a boundary interface. It can embody business rules or services. A PizzaMaker that controls the making of the Pizza() could exist between the PizzaOrdering() and a Pizza(). The PizzaMaker() would be a controller.

alters current_balance; mail_statement(), which mails the current_balance to the address; or is_credit_worthy(), which applies some business rules to determine whether to extend credit to the customer.

Let's take the PizzaOrdering interface in the first chapter and transform it into two interfaces on each end of the spectrum. First we make a pure DTO—a Pizza class containing just data on the pizza. For example:

```
class Pizza
    set_size(Size)
    set_topping(Topping)
    Size get_size()
    Topping [] get_toppings()
```

We now create a service interface that accepts a Pizza and places the order:

```
interface PizzaOrderer
    TimePeriod order_pizza(Pizza)
```

The method calling this interface first creates a Pizza and then passes the Pizza to order_pizza().

We can turn the Pizza class into a class endowed with more behavior, which is a guideline for object-oriented design. Let's add a method so that a Pizza orders itself:

```
class Pizza
    // as above, plus:
    order()
```

Pizza's order() method could call an implementation of the PizzaOrderer interface. One implementation could communicate the order over the telephone; another implementation could fax it or email it. The user of Pizza does not need to know about PizzaOrderer, unless they intend to change the implementation that order() uses.[2]

In Chapter 1, you ordered a pizza over the phone. If PizzaOrderer represented a phone-based system, before accessing order_pizza(), you need to call the shop. If we include that operation in this interface, it would look like this:

```
interface PizzaOrderer
    call_up()
    TimePeriod order_pizza(Pizza)
    hang_up()
```

Now PizzaOrderer represents a *service provider interface*, a variation of the service interface. A service provider adds methods to the interface that control the life cycle of the service provider. These methods are often called *initialize*, *start*, or *stop.* Java applets, servlets, and session beans are examples of service provider interfaces.

3.2 Data Access Interface Structures

You may run across different paradigms for interfaces that access data, so it's a good idea to appreciate the differences among them. An interface can provide sequential or random retrieval of data. Users can either pull data or have it pushed upon them.

---

[2]We explore ways to configure different implementations in Chapter 7.

Sequential versus Random Retrieval

Data can be available in a sequential or random manner. For example, the Java FileInputStream class allows only sequential access, while RandomAccessFile allows access to the data in a file in any order.

The same dichotomy exists within collections and iterators. An iterator interface allows access to a single element in a collection at a particular time. Some styles of iterators, such as Java's Iterator or C++'s forward iterators, permit only one-way access. You have to start at the beginning of the collection and continue in one direction to the end. On the other hand, a vector or array index, or a C++ random-access iterator, allows random access to any element in the set. If you have data available with only sequential access and you want it to have random access, you can build an adapter. For example, you can create a vector and fill it with the elements from an iterator.

Other examples of sequential vs. random access are two Java classes for accessing the data in an XML file. The Simple API for XML (SAX) parser provides for sequential access to the XML elements; SAX does not keep the data in memory. On the other hand, the Document Object Model (DOM) allows random access. It creates an in-memory representation of the XML data. Note that a DOM parser can use a SAX parser to help create the memory representation. These two interfaces have corresponding advantages and disadvantages.

SAX: SEQUENTIAL ACCESS

> Advantage—requires less resources to parse the file

> Disadvantage—application cannot change the XML data

DOM: RANDOM ACCESS

> Advantage—application can change the XML data

> Disadvantage—requires memory to store the entire document

We'll revisit SAX and DOM in a little more detail in a later section.

Pull and Push Interfaces

Interfaces move data in one of two ways: push or pull. You ask a pull-style interface—for example, a web browser—for data. Whenever you desire information, you type in a URL, and the information is returned. On the other hand, a push-style interface transfers data to you. An email subscription is a push-style interface. Your mail program receives information whenever the mail subscription program sends new mail. You don't ask for it; you just get it.

You can use either a pull style or a push style when going through a collection.[3] An example of a pull style is the typical iteration through a list or array:

```
Item an_item
for_each an_item in a_list
    {
    an_item.print()
    }
```

For each element in a_list, the print() method is explicitly called. The push style for this operation is as follows:

```
print_item(Item passed_item)
    {
    passed_item.print()
    }
a.list.for_each(print_item)
```

The for_each() method iterates through a_list. For each item, for_each() calls the print_item() method, which is passed the current item on the list.

For each language, the actual code for the push style is different. For example, in C++, you can use the for_each() function in the Standard Template Library (STL). With this function, each item in the vector is pushed to the print_item() function.

```
void print_item(Item item)
  {
  cout << item <<' ';
  }
vector <Item> a_list;
for_each(a_list.begin(), a_list.end(), print_item);
```

In Ruby, the code could be as follows:

```
a_list = [1,2,3]
a_list.each { |passed_item| passeditem.print_item()}.
```

PUSH STYLE

Advantage—can be simpler code, once paradigm is understood

---

[3]*Design Patterns* refers to pull and push styles for a collection as *internal* and *external* iterators.

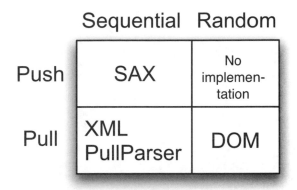

Figure 3.2: EXAMPLES OF DATA INTERFACES

PULL STYLE

Advantage—appears as a common control style (e.g., loop) in multiple languages

One from Each Column

Pull/push style and sequential/random styles can be intermixed in combinations. As an example of a set of combinations in a specific area, let's revisit XML parsing. SAX is push/sequential; DOM is pull/random. There is also a pull-style sequential interface called XMLPull-Parser.[4]

Figure 3.2 shows how these three styles relate. The "No implementation" box shows a variation for which no current implementation exists.[5] Depending on what elements you want to retrieve from an XML file, what you want to do with the elements, and memory constraints, you choose one of these interface styles to create simpler code. To compare how you might employ each of these versions, let's take a look at some logic in pseudocode. In each of these examples, we print the count for one element in an XML file. The XML file looks like this:

---

[4]See http://www.xmlpull.org/v1/doc/api/org/xmlpull/v1/XmlPullParser. html for full details.

[5]We can't think of a need for this variation, so that may be why no one has created one.

```
<order>
    <pizza>
        <topping>
        Pepperoni
        </topping>
        <topping>
        Mushroom
        </topping>
    </pizza>
    <icecream>
        <topping>
        Whipped Cream
        </topping>
    </icecream>
</order>
```

We want to print how many times the topping tag appears for a pizza. To concentrate on the logic, we'll ignore error handling and a few other details. The pseudocode for the push/sequential SAX parser looks like this:

```
SAXParser sax = new SAXParser('file.xml');
sax.setContentHandler(new MyContentHandler());
sax.parse()
```

parse() reads the XML file. Every time parse() finds an XML tag, it invokes the appropriate method in MyContentHandler. MyContentHandler does not control the flow of method calls. It just provides the methods that are called by parse(). The pseudocode for MyContentHandler looks like:

```
class MyContentHandler
    boolean foundPizza = false
    int count = 0
    startElement(String localName)
        if (localName == "pizza")
            count = 0
            foundPizza = true
        if (foundPizza && (localName == "topping") )
            count++
    endElement(String localName)
        if (localName == "pizza")
            foundPizza = false
            print count
```

When a start tag is found by parse(), it calls startElement(). startElement() needs to keep track of the place in the document it was invoked. It does so by using foundPizza. This ensures that only toppings that are associated with a pizza are counted.

On the other hand, DOM reads the entire XML file and constructs an object tree. Then you access the tree in whatever order you desire. The pseudocode for DOM looks like this:

```
DOMParser dom = new DOMParser()
dom.parse('file.xml')
Document document = dom.getDocument()
```

At this point, the document is completely parsed. You access the elements by calling methods in the Node class. For example, the method getElementsByTagName() retrieves all the tags with a given name. The pseudocode looks like:

```
Node [] thePizzas = document.getElementsByTagName("pizza")
for each Node in thePizzas
    Node [] theToppings = node.getElementsByTagName("topping")
    print length of theTopping
```

With XMLPullParser, you move through the XML document in a sequential manner. Unlike the SAXParser, you ask the parser to give you the next token. You then ask the token for its type. The pseudocode for handling the parsed data looks like this:

```
XMLPullParser xml = new XMLPullParser('file.xml')
while true
    int event = parser.nextToken()
    if (event == XmlPullParser.END_DOCUMENT)
        break
    if ((event == XmlPullParser.START_TAG) &&
        (parser.getName() == "pizza"))
            int count = 0
        while (true)
            event = parser.nextToken();
            if ((event == XmlPullParser.START_TAG) &&
                (parser.getName() == "topping"))
                    count ++;
            if ((event ==  XmlPullParser.END_TAG) &&
                (parser.getName() == "pizza"))
                    print count
                    break
```

Although the XMLPullParser code is longer than the other two examples, the flow may be familiar to more programmers. You track where you are in the document by which line of code you are executing.

Making general statements about combinations of interface styles is difficult; you need to experience how you are going to use the combination. For the specific instance of XML parsing, to the advantages and

Asynchronous Pushing

Push methods may be called asynchronously. The Observer pattern as commonly used in graphical user interfaces (GUIs) is an example of asynchronous pushing. You provide a method that is called when a button is clicked or a mouse hovers over a widget such as a text box. The method may be called at any time. Java's ActionListener is an example of this Observer pattern. When a button is clicked, the actionPerformed( ) is called. If you have multiple buttons on the screen, any one of them could be clicked at any time. Your program needs to be able to handle the buttons in any order. The issues with dealing with randomly ordered events are a topic for another book.

disadvantages previously mentioned for sequential/random dichotomy of SAX and DOM, we could add these:

SAX—SEQUENTIAL ACCESS/PUSH

Disadvantage—user must keep track of previous events

DOM—RANDOM ACCESS/PULL

Advantage—simple to find particular elements

XMLPULLPARSER—SEQUENTIAL ACCESS/PULL

Advantage—flow may be familiar to more programmers

Disadvantage—may have more code than the other two alternatives

3.3 Alternative Interfaces

You always face the problem of how to embody particular features in an interface. You typically have at least two ways to structure a particular feature. Let's look at some of the issues involved in selecting a design.

Suppose you are creating an interface for a simple formatted document. For example:

```
interface FormattedDocument
    add_text(String)
```

You want to add the ability to format the text with either underlining or bold attributes. You have at least two options for the methods: first, you could use separate methods:

```
set_bold()
set_italic()
set_underline()
```

Second, you could have a single method with a parameter:

```
enumeration FontModifier { BOLD, ITALIC, UNDERLINE, NORMAL }
set_font_modifier(FontModifier)
```

The behavior in both these cases is the same—each method alters the appearance of the formatted text.[6] With only three font modifiers, the trade-off between the two versions does not weigh heavily one way or the other. In the first version, the method call is shorter, but you have more methods. However, the second interface can be more resilient to change. If you add a STRIKETHOUGH modifier, the method signatures of the implementers do not have to change. Previous versions of the set_font_modifier() method will not output STRIKETHROUGH, but they may fail gracefully.

A similar trade-off occurs with the Observer pattern. In our example from Chapter 2, we had two methods for the CustomerObserver. They were the following:

```
interface CustomerObserver
    notify_address_change(address)
    notify_name_change(name)
```

If you add another event to the interface (say notify_balance_change()), you have to change all the places where this interface is implemented. Instead, you could cut down the interface to a single method. The method could provide an indicator of what has changed, like this:

```
interface CustomerObserver
    enumeration ChangeType {ADDRESS, NAME}
    notify_change(ChangeType value)
```

If you add BALANCE to ChangeType, you do not have to change any observers. Alternatively, you might have the method pass the new and old values:

```
interface CustomerObserver
    notify_change(Customer old_customer, Customer new_customer)
```

---

[6]The two sets of methods differ on a more subtle level. A reviewer noted that the definition of each alternative method did not specify whether the other font modifiers were reset. For example, does calling set_bold() turn off all the other modifiers, or do you need unset() methods? If set_font_modifier() allowed for multiple modifiers (e.g., BOLD and ITALIC), then its contract could be to turn off all other modifiers.

The observer would need to determine what the differences between the old_customer and the new_customer were. But now you would not have to change CustomerObserver at all.

MANY METHODS

Advantage—implementer does not have to determine type of parameter

Disadvantage—implementer has to implement all the methods

SINGLE METHODS

Advantage—can be more resilient to change, because new methods do not have to be implemented

Disadvantage—must check parameter type to determine flow

This trade-off appears in listener interfaces in Java that are observer interfaces for many of the GUI widgets. For example, to listen to events occurring in a window, you must implement WindowListener. This interface contains many methods:

```
interface WindowListener
    {
    windowActivated(WindowEvent)
    windowClosed(WindowEvent)
    windowClosing(WindowEvent)
    windowDeactivated(WindowEvent)
    windowDeiconified(WindowEvent)
    windowIconified(WindowEvent)
    windowOpened(WindowEvent)
    }
```

A listener knows what event has occurred by which method is called. The parameter that is passed is needed only for the details of the event, not the type of event.

You may be interested in only one of the events, but you still need to code a body for all the methods in the interface. This can be annoying, so Java supplies a WindowListenerAdapter, which is really a WindowListener with default method bodies. Each method body does nothing. If your class inherits from WindowListenerAdapter, it needs to override the methods only for the events for which you are interested.

In this configuration, you really have not inherited an implementation. You have just overcome a constraint of the language that requires a class to implement all methods in an interface. The Java listener interface could have been designed differently. There could have been multiple interfaces, like this:

```
interface WindowClosedListener
    {
    windowClosed(WindowEvent)
    }
interface windowIconifiedListener
    {
    windowIconified (WindowEvent)
    }
```

If you wanted to listen to only a single event, you would need to implement only a single method. You would not need a WindowListenerAdapter.

In C# and Ruby, the callback method equivalent to windowClosed() does not need to be part of an interface.[7] The method can simply be any one that matches the signature for a callback method. For example, in Ruby, you hook up a listener for the window-closed event with the following:

```
root = TkRoot.new()
frame = TkFrame.new(root)
frame.bind('Destroy') { puts 'Window Closed' }
```

The code following `frame.bind` is executed when the window is destroyed.

3.4 Stateless versus Stateful Interfaces

An interface implementation can either contain state (stateful) or not contain state (stateless). In a stateful interface, the methods operate differently based on the current state, which is changed by the sequence of method invocations. In a stateless interface, the behavior is not dependent on the history of method invocations. Its behavior is always the same. A stateful versus stateless PizzaFinder service illustrates the difference. Let's examine the trade-offs between these two types. Along the way, we'll see how a stateful interface can be adapted to a stateless one.[8]

Imagine if I were to call my mother and ask her to find the number for Tony's Pizza. She looks it up and says, "Well, there are five." I say, "Thanks, Mom, please give me the first one." I hang up and call it only to find out they don't deliver to my neighborhood. I can call up my mom

---

[7]In C#, the keyword **delegate** is used to denote the signature of a callback method. In Ruby, there are no interface declarations.

[8]Thanks to David Bock for providing this example.

and say, "Hi, Mom, please give me the next one." She can then respond with the next one. The conversation with my mother has state. She remembers that I had asked about Tony's Pizza and where I was in the list.

Contrast this to calling the operator. I ask for the first Tony's Pizza on the list; they respond; I call, and it isn't the right one. If I call back information and say, "Give me the next," the operator will say, "Next one what, sir? I don't know what you are talking about." The conversation with the operator is stateless. I will have to tell the operator on the second phone call that I am calling about Tony's Pizza, and I want the second one in the list.

STATELESS

Advantage—a small number of operators can service many requests. My mom would not be able to juggle more than a few requestors at a time.

STATEFUL

Advantage—there is less chatter to get the same amount of work done.

Let's look at some program examples of stateful and stateless interfaces. We introduced programming a GUI in Chapter 1. In most languages, you have the equivalent of a GraphicsContext interface that contains the state of the current font modifiers (e.g., BOLD). Suppose you want to write a series of text with different modifiers. With a stateful interface, you might code the equivalent of this:

```
GraphicsContext graphics_context;
graphics_context.set_font_modifier(BOLD)
graphics_context.print_text('In Bold')
graphics_context.print_text('Also in Bold')
graphics_context.set_font_modifier(ITALIC)
graphics_context.print_text('In Italics');
```

You first set the graphics_context to print in BOLD, which alters the state of the GraphicsContext. All text from that point is printed in BOLD, until the state of the graphic context is set to ITALIC.

The opposite form—a stateless interface—requires that you specify all the font information in each call. The interface does not keep track of the font modifiers. Calls to a stateless interface would look like this:

```
graphics_context.print_text(BOLD, 'In Bold')
graphics_context.print_text(BOLD, 'Also in Bold')
graphics_context.print_text(ITALIC, 'In Italics')
```

> ## Consistency
>
> If you're creating an interface, you should be consistent in your parameter placement. You may have noticed that drawstring() and TextOut() have parameter lists that are reversed. Similarly, the parameter lists to create a font are reversed. Which one is correct? Take a poll of your fellow programmers, and see whether there is a preference.
>
> I don't have a definitive guideline other than being as consistent as possible with the other interfaces you use in your organization.

STATELESS

> Advantage—order of the method calls does not matter
>
> Disadvantage—parameter lists are longer

STATEFUL

> Advantage—parameter lists shorter
>
> Disadvantage—order of method calls important

If you move the call to `set_font_modifier(ITALIC)` down one line in the stateful example, then "In Italics" prints in bold. You can alter the sequence of calls in the stateless interface, and the text is always printed with the same font modifier.

The graphics contexts for Java and MFC (Graphics and CDC, respectively) are stateful. The state includes values such as the current font (e.g., Times Roman) for text output and the foreground and background color of text. In both frameworks, you set the font, and then subsequent drawing is in that font. In this Java example, graphics is the graphics context:

```
Font font = new Font('Times-Roman',12)
graphics.setFont(font);
graphics.drawString('Hello world', 200, 300);
```

MFC works in a similar fashion. The graphics context is represented with a pointer, pDC.

```
CFont font;
font.CreateFont(12,'Times-Roman');
pDC->SelectObject(&font);
pDC->TextOut(200,300,'Hello world');
```

These graphics context methods eventually wind up calling methods in Windows' Graphics Display Interface (GDI), such as DrawText(). The GDI methods then call methods in the Display Driver Interface (DDI), such as DrvTextOut(). This function sends text out to a device. Here are some of the relevant parameters:[9]

```
BOOL DrvTextOut( STROBJ * pointer_string_object,
    FONTOBJ * pointer_font_object,
    RECTL * pointer_opaque_rectangle );
```

This interface is stateless. The GDI passes everything that is needed— the font in which to render the text (pointer_font_object), the position at which to write the text (pointer_opaque_rectangle), and the text itself (pointer_string_object). The current state of the graphics context is used to fill in those parameters. So, the stateful interface of Java and MFC invokes the stateful interface of GDI, which then executes the stateless DDI. A stateful interface is transformed into a stateless one.[10] This statelessness simplifies coding of the device driver. It does not have to remember "and what font was I printing in?"

Each device driver provides an implementation of the methods such as DrvTextOut(). For a printer, the driver implementation converts the information into a type specific to that particular printer. The driver could output the text in PostScript or Hewlett Packard's Printer Control Language (PCL). Or the driver could create a bitmap of the text in the processor and output that bitmap to the printer. The details of each printer are opaque to the user of the Java or MFC interface.

If the output to the printer is a PostScript file, then the driver has created a textual interface from a procedural one. So, the flow goes from a stateful procedural interface at the user level to a stateless procedural interface at the driver level to a textual interface. This sort of conversion from one type of interface to another is common in many systems.

3.5 Transformation Considerations

"If you can't be with the one you love, love the one you're with," wrote Stephen Stills. You don't have to love an interface you're given. If you don't like way that an interface works, transform it into one you like.

---

[9]You can find the full interface at http://msdn.microsoft.com.

[10]A device driver may keep internal state to improve performance, but callers of the interface do not rely upon that fact or even know it.

Nonobject Interface into Object Interface

Let's examine a few ways that the Unix input/output interface can be transformed into an object-oriented interface. In Chapters 1 and 2, we presented the File interface:

```
interface File
    open(filename, flags) signals UnableToOpen
    read(buffer, count) signals EndOfFile, UnableToRead
    write(buffer, count) signals UnableToWrite
    close()
```

An implementation of this interface—such as MyFile—has a private instance variable that represents the common element (the file_descriptor) of the original C functions:

```
class MyFile implements File
    private file_descriptor
    open(filename, flags) signals UnableToOpen
    read(buffer, count) signals EndOfFile, UnableToRead
    write(buffer, count) signals UnableToWrite
    close()
```

This straightforward translation of the original functionality raises an interesting question as to the protocol for the interface. Should you have a class that allows for possibly invalid instances? For example, you could create an instance of the MyFile type without it being connected to an open file. Then other methods (e.g., read(), write()) should check the state and not attempt to perform an operation on an unopened file.

On the other hand, if a File object should exist only in the open state, then a constructor should assume the functionality of the open method. The destructor can perform the closing of the file. Objects that cannot exist in an invalid state can make it easier to check the preconditions and postconditions that were covered in Chapter 2.

A class with a constructor looks like this:

```
class FileWithConstructor
    private file_descriptor
    FileWithConstructor(filename, flags) signals UnableToOpen
    read(buffer, count) signals EndOfFile, UnableToRead
    write(buffer, count) signals UnableToWrite
    destructor()
```

The FileWithConstructor class can implement a different interface, such as FileAlwaysOpen. For example:

```
interface FileAlwaysOpen
    read(buffer, count) signals EndOfFile, UnableToRead
    write(buffer, count) signals UnableToWrite
```

Use a factory method to make use of this interface more opaque:

```
interface FileAlwaysOpenFactory
    FileAlwaysOpen get_file(filename, flags) signals UnableToOpen
```

Inside the get_file() method, you create an instance of FileWithConstructor, which implements the FileAlwaysOpen interface. The pseudocode for the interface looks like this:

```
FileAlwaysOpen get_file(filename, flags) signals UnableToOpen
return new FileWithConstructor(filename, flags)
```

Note that the parameters to the get_file() method are the same as the parameters for the constructor. You could always create a FileWithConstructor directly:

```
FileAlwaysOpen file = new FileWithConstructor('myfile.txt', READ_ONLY);
```

More Specific Interfaces

We discussed in Chapter 1 that you might want to send specialized commands to particular types of devices. The Unix/Linux ioctl() method and textual interfaces are two ways of sending device-specific commands. To hide the details of communication, you could create device-specific interfaces. The methods in the interface are applicable to only a single device. For example, for a modem, you might have the following:

```
interface ModemDevice
  hangup()
  dial_phone_number(PhoneNumber) signals NoAnswer, NoDialTone, NoCarrier
    // sends 'ATDT' + PhoneNumber to modem
```

The dial_phone_number() method sends the "ATDT" string, as shown in Chapter 1. The user of this interface does not need to remember the specific command string.

With the general FileAlwaysOpen factory, you could perhaps create a FileAlwaysOpen and then ensure that it is a ModemDevice before you try to dial a number with it. For example:

```
FileAlwaysOpen a_stream= FileAlwaysOpenFactory.get_file('/dev/mdm',
  READ_WRITE);
if (a_stream is_a ModemDevice)
    (ModemDevice) a_stream.dial_phone_number('5551212')
```

Alternatively, you could create a more specific factory method that returns only a device that implements the ModemDevice interface. For example:

```
class Modem implements FileAlwaysOpen, ModemDevice

Modem m = ModemFactory.get_modem();
m.dial_phone_number(' 5551212' );
```

You could make an interface that parallels the "never invalid" concept of FileAlwaysOpen. In this case, ModemDevice is hidden. The factory always returns an instance of a dialed number.

```
class PhoneConnectionAlwaysOpen implements FileAlwaysOpen

interface PhoneConnectionFactory
    PhoneConnectionAlwaysOpen  get_phone_connection(PhoneNumber)
        signals NoAnswer, NoDialTone, NoCarrier

PhoneConnectionAlwaysOpen m =
    PhoneConnectionFactory.get_phone_connection(' 5551212' );
```

Transforming Textual Interfaces to Programmatic Interfaces

Like the modem commands, you can transform most textual interfaces into an interface with methods. For example, the File Transfer Protocol (FTP) mentioned in Chapter 1 has commands such as the following:

```
open hostname #Open a connection
get filename #Get a file
close #Close a connection
```

You can transform these commands into a method interface by creating methods for each command with the appropriate parameters and the appropriate error signals. For example:

```
interface FTPService
    open(hostname, username, password) signals
        UnableToConnect, IncorrectUsernameOrPassword
    get(filename) signals NoSuchFile, UnableToCommunicate
    close()
```

On the server, the textual commands received from the client can be transformed into method calls against a similar interface. The service directory example in Chapter 9 gives another example of converting from a method interface to a textual interface and back again.

DEVICE SPECIFIC
    Advantage—hides device/protocol implementation issues

3.6 Multiple Interfaces

You are not stuck with a one-to-one relationship between an interface and a module. A module can implement more than one interface. When you implement multiple interfaces, you may have interface collision problems. As an example, we'll look at a pizza shop that also sells ice cream.

Ice Cream Interface

You're hungry for an ice cream cone. The PizzaOrdering interface doesn't allow you to order ice cream. So, you find an implementation of an IceCreamOrdering interface that appears as follows:

```
enumeration Flavor { Chocolate, Vanilla, Coffee,Strawberry, ..}
enumeration ConeType { Sugar, Waffle}
interface IceCreamOrdering
    set_number_scoops(Count)
    set_cone_type(ConeType)
    set_flavors(Flavor [])
```

Now an ice cream–only shop may implement the IceCreamOrderingin-terface. On the other hand, a shop that offers the PizzaOrdering interface may also offer the IceCreamOrdering interface. To do so, the shop must provide an implementation of all methods in both interfaces as:

```
enumeration Toppings {PEPPERONI, MUSHROOMS, PEPPERS, SAUSAGE}
class CombinedPizzaIceCreamShop implements PizzaOrdering
  and IceCreamOrdering
    set_number_scoops(Count)
    set_cone_type(ConeType)
    set_flavors(Flavor [])
    set_size(Size)
    set_toppings(Toppings [])
    set_address(String street_address)
    TimePeriod get_time_till_delivered()
```

Trying to implement multiple interfaces can lead to some interesting issues. Suppose that IceCreamOrdering also had a set_toppings() method:

```
enumeration Toppings {WHIP_CREAM, CHERRY, CHOCOLATE_JIMMIES, PINEAPPLE}
set_toppings(Toppings [])
```

If the Toppings enumeration contained all the choices for both pizzas and ice cream, then set_toppings() would need to differentiate between which item was being ordered. Otherwise, you might get sausage on your ice cream. With most languages, the enumeration of Toppings for IceCream and Pizza can be placed in its own namespace (e.g., in a module or package). So, CombinedPizzaIceCreamShop would implement two methods that took different Topping enumerations:

```
set_toppings(PizzaOrdering.Toppings [])
set_toppings(IceCreamOrdering.Toppings [])
```

If the methods took more primitive parameters (e.g., String or double), then differentiating them would be harder. For example, suppose you had the following interface methods:

```
interface PizzaOrdering
    set_toppings(String toppings)
interface IceCreamOrdering
    set_toppings(String toppings)
```

then the combined shop could have only a single method:[11]

```
class CombinedPizzaIceCreamShop implements PizzaOrdering
  and IceCreamOrdering
    set_toppings(String toppings)
```

The set_toppings() method has to be a bit more complicated to handle both ice cream and pizza toppings, or else you might be eating chocolate syrup on your pizza or pepperoni on your vanilla cone.[12]

3.7 Things to Remember

We've looked at several key ingredients in creating interfaces, and we explored the spectrum between data and service interfaces. When designing code, keep in mind the advantages and disadvantages of several approaches to interfaces:

- Sequential versus random data access

- Push versus pull interfaces

- Stateful versus stateless interfaces

- Multiple methods versus single methods

A module may implement multiple interfaces by providing method implementations for all of the methods. You can transform interfaces from non-object-oriented code to object-oriented interfaces and textual interfaces into procedural-style interfaces.

---

[11]C# permits overriding methods that have the same signature if they appear in different interfaces.

[12]I'm sure there is someone somewhere who reads that and goes, "Wow, what a great idea!" Let me know if you are this someone, so I can avoid having to watch you eat.

Chapter 4

What Should Be in an Interface?

One of the most difficult decisions in developing a program is determining what should be in an interface. The oft-quoted guideline for object-oriented programming is that classes should be cohesive and loosely coupled. In this chapter, we'll see how these two concepts apply to interfaces.

You often face another question: how many methods should you have in an interface? Many methods can make an interface more difficult to understand but can also make it more powerful. We will explore the trade-offs in minimal to complete interfaces.

4.1 Cohesiveness

Methods in an interface should be cohesive. They should provide services that revolve around a common concept.[1] The problem is that the definition of commonness is relative. For example, a share of stock is a liability to a corporation, an asset to the owner, and something to sell for a broker. According to Flood and Carson, the United Kingdom "could be seen as an economy by economists, a society by sociologists, a threaded chunk of nature by conservationists, a tourist attraction by some Americans, a military threat by rulers of the Soviet Union, and the green, green grass of home to the more romantic of us Britons."[2]

---

[1]The cohesion quality predates object-oriented programming. An original reference is W.P. Stevens, G.J. Myers, and L.L. Constantine's, "Structured Design", *IBM Systems Journal*, Vol. 13, No. 2, 1974.

[2]See *Dealing with Complexity* by Robert Flood and Ewart Carons (Plenum Press, 1988).

> **What Sticks Together?**
> _____
>
> I had a psychology professor who gave exams that were
> designed to make you fail. He would give four terms and
> ask the question, how many of these go together? Well, it
> all depended on how you interpreted "go together." He col-
> lected all the exams, so I don't have an example. But let me
> give you one from programming. These are programming lan-
> guages: Fortran, C, C++, and Java. How many of these lan-
> guages relate to one another? a.) Two, b.) Three, c.) Four, d.)
> None
>
> If you and your team agree on an answer, then you probably
> share a common approach to cohesiveness.

You can find commonness in almost anything. For example, "Why is a lightbulb like Doonesbury?" Neither one can whistle.

We're going to look at the interface to a printer to demonstrate a range of cohesiveness. Depending on your point of view, you might consider that all printer operations belong in one interface, since they are all related to printing. Or you might consider a narrower view of cohesiveness that divides the operations into multiple interfaces.[3]

4.2 A Printer Interface

You have a number of different printers in your office; each of them has different capabilities. Let's create a spreadsheet that shows the different features for each printer. You probably can think of many more capabilities, but we need to have the table fit onto a single printed page. In Figure 4.1, on the next page, a check mark indicates that a printer performs a particular operation.

Suppose you were to create your own printing subsystem. The question is, how do you place these capabilities into interfaces? Do you have a single interface or multiple ones? You need to determine which capabilities are available when printing a page. For example, if the printer has the capability to turn over the page, you want to ask the user whether

------

[3]For a look at eight kinds of cohesion (from Functional Cohesion to Coincidental), see `http://elearning.tvm.tcs.co.in/SDO/SDO/3_3.htm`.

Function/ Printer	print_ text	eject_ page	print_ color_ image	print_ bw_ image	turn_ over_ page	which_ side_are_ you_on	get_ trays	select_ tray	print_ postscript	print_ pclt
Model1	✔	✔	✔	✔						
Model2	✔	✔			✔	✔				
Model3	✔	✔		✔					✔	
Model4	✔	✔		✔	✔	✔	✔	✔		✔

Figure 4.1: Printer feature matrix

they want double sided printing. If it has the capability to print a black-and-white image but not a color one, you may want to convert a color image to black and white before printing it.

You could place methods for all these operations into a single interface. Every printer has methods for all operations, but a method does nothing for an operation that the printer does not perform. If the printer is unable to perform an operation, the method should signal that it couldn't. Otherwise, the method violates the spirit of the Third Law of Interfaces presented in Chapter 2 ("Notify callers if unable to perform"). The interface might look like this:

```
interface Printer
    print_text(Position, Font, String)
    eject_page()
    print_image_in_color(Position, Image)
    print_image_in_black_and_white(Position, Image)
    turn_over_page()
    Side which_side_are_you_on()
    select_tray(TrayID)
    TrayID [] get_tray_ids()
    print_postscript(PostscriptString)
    print_pcl(PCLString)
```

Corresponding to each capability method, the interface could also have a method that indicates whether it is capable of performing an operation. This would honor the spirit of the First Law of Interfaces ("Do what the methods say they do"). For example, the interface would have methods like the following:

```
Boolean can_turn_over_page()
Boolean can_print_pcl()
```

Similar to the set_font_modifier() method in Chapter 3, these multiple methods could be turned into a single one, like this:[4]

```
enumeration Operation {TURN_OVER_PAGE, PRINT_PCL,...}
Boolean can_perform(Operation)
```

Your printing subsystem asks the printer whether it can perform a particular operation before calling the corresponding method:

```
printing_subsystem (Printer a_printer)
    if (a_printer.can_perform(TURN_OVER_PAGE)
        // ask user if they want duplex printing
```

A second way to organize the model/feature table is to break up the methods into multiple interfaces. Each interface consists of a related set of methods. A particular printer model implements only the interfaces for which it has capabilities. For example, the printer interfaces could be as follows:

```
interface BasicPrinter
    print_text(Position, Font, String)
    eject_page()
interface ColorPrinter
    print_image_in_color(Position, Image)
    print_image_in_black_and_white(Position, Image)
interface MonochromePrinter
    print_image_black_and_white(Position, Image)
interface DoubleSidedPrinter
    turn_over_page()
    Side which_side_on_you_on()
interface MultiTrayPrinter
    select_tray(TrayID)
    TrayID [] get_tray_ids()
interface PostscriptPrinter
    print_postscript(PostscriptString)
interface PCLPrinter
    print_pcl(PCLString)
```

How do we decide what operations to put into what interface? It's a matter of cohesiveness. If the operations (e.g., turn_over_page() and which_side_are_you_on()) will be used together, they should go into the same interface. If printers always supply operations as a set, then they should go together.

The single Printer interface collects all operations relating to printers. So, you may consider it a cohesive interface. On the other hand, each

---

[4]Note that in Windows you can call the capability method, GetDeviceCaps(), to ask whether a particular operation is supported. For example, GetDeviceCaps(TEXTCAPS) returns a value indicating text capabilities, such as TC_UA_ABLE (can underline).

of these specialized interfaces has methods relating only to a particular capability. So, you might think of them as more cohesive. Note that a printer does not need to have any knowledge of interfaces it cannot provide.[5] We do not have to ask a printer "can you do this for me?" for each operation. We see that a printer can do something by the fact that it implements an interface.

Before we move on, let's quickly look at how you might find a particular type of printer. A printer provides an implementation of one or more of the interfaces. For example:

```
class MySpecialPrinter implements BasicPrinter, ColorPrinter,
    MultiTrayPrinter
```

You can provide a method that lets the user find a printer that implements a particular interface. For example, they may want to find one that can print in color. So, the user codes the following:

```
my_printing_method()
    {
    ColorPrinter a_printer = (ColorPrinter)
        PrinterCollection.find(ColorPrinter)
    a_printer.print_image_in_color(position, image)
    }
```

Now what if you want to pass around just a reference to a BasicPrinter, and inside a method you wanted to use it as a ColorPrinter? You could simply cast the reference to a ColorPrinter. If it did not implement the interface, then a cast exception would be thrown:

```
a_function (BasicPrinter a_printer) throws CastException
    {
    ColorPrinter color = (ColorPrinter) a_printer
    color.print_image_in_color(position, image)
    }
```

If you really needed to find out whether the printer had more capabilities, you could ask it whether it implements a desired interface. This is the equivalent of testing for capabilities (e.g., calling can_perform() for Printer) but for a related set of capabilities.[6]

---

[5]An alternative is to have a base class, ComprehensivePrinter, that implements all interfaces but has null operations for most of the methods. Then each printer inherits from ComprehensivePrinter. We look at inheritance in Chapter 5.

[6]The code looks like *downcasting* (casting a base class to a derived class). You should usually avoid downcasting. In this example, the cast is to an interface, rather than a derived class.

```
a_function (BasicPrinter a_printer)
    {
    if (a_printer is_a ColorPrinter)
        {
        ColorPrinter color = (ColorPrinter) a_printer
        color.print_image_in_color(position, image)
        }
    }
```

However, if a_function() really required a ColorPrinter, it should be passed a reference to one, rather than having to test for it. That makes its contract explicit. The cast exception will occur when the reference is passed.

```
a_function (ColorPrinter a_printer)
    {
    a_printer.print_image_in_color(position, image)
    }
```

SINGLE PRINTER INTERFACE
    Advantage—can have single capability query method

    Disadvantage—related capabilities may not be logically grouped together

MULTIPLE PRINTER INTERFACES
    Advantage—printer need only implement interfaces it supplies

    Disadvantage—lots of interfaces

4.3 Coupling

Coupling measures how one module depends on the implementation of another module. A method that depends upon the internal implementation of a class is tightly coupled to that class. If that implementation changes, then you have to alter the method. Too much coupling—especially when it's not necessary—leads to brittle systems that are hard to extend and maintain.

But if you rely on interfaces instead, then it's difficult to tightly couple a method to another implementation. A method that just calls the methods in another interface is loosely coupled to that interface. If you simply use a reference to an interface implementation without calling any methods, then the two are considered really loosely coupled.

In the printer example, my_printing_method() is loosely coupled to Color-Printer and PrinterCollection:

> ### Who's Job Is It Anyway?
>
> You probably have printed digital photographs. Printing a digital photograph brings up an interesting question: if you want to print an image in a resolution different from the printer's resolution, where should you assign the job of converting the image to a different resolution?
>
> You have two options:
>
> - Pass the printer driver the image, and let it perform its own resolution conversion (perhaps by calling a graphics library).
>
> - Ask the printer for the resolution it can handle, convert the image to that resolution, and pass the converted image to the printer.
>
> You might say, what's the difference? The result should be the same. Maybe, maybe not. This is where the quality of implementation comes into play. The program that you are using to print the image may have a much higher quality of resolution conversion than the graphics library. The developers may have done a better job in reducing conversion artifacts.
>
> Although you may often trust the implementation of an interface to do the right thing, you may want to perform your own set of processing to ensure that you get exactly what you want. This quality of implementation issue sometimes makes it hard to determine what is the appropriate job for an interface.

```
my_printing_method()
    ColorPrinter a_printer = (ColorPrinter)
        PrinterCollection.find(ColorPrinter)
    a_printer.print_image_in_color(position, image)
```

If this method did not call a method in ColorPrinter, then it would be really loosely coupled. For example, it could simply pass the reference to another method, as:

```
my_printing_method()
    ColorPrinter a_printer = (ColorPrinter)
        PrinterCollection.find(ColorPrinter)
    print_some_color_image(a_printer, position, image);
```

Loose coupling allows you to vary the implementation of the called interface without having to change the code that calls it. On the other hand, tight coupling forces the code to change. Here's a silly example to show tight coupling:

```
class Pizza
    wake_up_johnny
    order
```

In this example, Johnny is the implementation of the order taker. He needs to be woken up before he can take an order. If Johnny leaves and Sam takes over, Sam may be able to stay awake. The wake_up_johnny() method would go away, forcing any code that calls the method to be altered. The solution is to decouple the implementation by using an interface and hiding the implementation. For example:

```
interface Pizza
    order

class PizzaWithJohnny implements Pizza
    order
        calls wake_up_johnny
        and then performs regular order
```

TIGHT COUPLING
> Disadvantage—callers have to be changed if implementation changes

LOOSE COUPLING
> Advantage—callers do not need to be changed if implementation changes

4.4 Interface Measures

Interfaces can be subjectively measured on a number of scales. Let's look at two of these measures: minimal versus complete and simple versus complex. An interface you design or use can fall anywhere in these ranges.

Minimal versus Complete

A minimal or sufficient interface has just the methods that a caller needs to perform their work cases. A complete interface has more methods. The File interface in Chapter 3 had the following:

```
interface File
    open(filename, flags) signals UnableToOpen
    read(buffer, count) signals EndOfFile, UnableToRead
    write(buffer, count) signals UnableToWrite
    close()
```

You might note that the interface does not have a skip() method. This method would allow a caller to skip over a number of bytes so that they do not have to read the intermediate bytes. A caller who needs to skip some number of bytes can simply read that many bytes and ignore them. If a caller wants to go backward, they can close the file, open it again, and start reading from the desired position.[7] The interface is sufficient for a user to perform the needed functionality.

On the other extreme, a caller might want the File interface to have additional methods, like these:

```
read_a_line()
find_a_regular_expression(expression)
```

Adding these methods makes the interface more complete, in the sense that it will have all the potential methods that a user might need. However, a more complete interface becomes more difficult to implement, because of the number of methods. An alternative is to create another interface with these methods, like this:

```
interface FileCharacterReader
    read_a_line()
    find_a_regular_expression(expression)
```

This interface would use an implementation of the minimal File interface for the read() method and add the logic to return the appropriate set of characters. Creating this interface can also help with cohesiveness. You can place methods that treat a File as a set of characters in FileCharacterReader.

MINIMAL

Advantage—easier to implement and test with fewer methods

Disadvantage—user must code their particular functionality and may wind up with duplicate code for same functionality

COMPLETE

Advantage—user has all needed methods

Disadvantage—may be harder to understand an interface with numerous methods

---

[7]A skip() method would probably be more efficient if it were implemented as part of the interface.

Simplicity versus Complexity

If you were making a pizza yourself, rather than ordering one, you might have a class like this:

```
class SimplePizza
    set_size(Size)
    set_topping(Topping)
    Size get_size()
    Topping [] get_toppings()
    make()
```

At the completion of the make() method, a SimplePizza is ready for your eating pleasure.

You could have a more complex interface, such as this:

```
class PizzaYourWay
    set_size(Size)
    set_topping(Topping)
    Size get_size()
    Topping [] get_toppings()
    mix_dough()
    spin()
    place_toppings(Topping [])
    bake()
    slice()
```

PizzaYourWay allows you to control the pizza-making process with more precision. You could slice() the pizza before you place_toppings() and then bake() the pizza. If you were splitting the pizza with a vegetarian, you would not get the artichoke juice mixed in with your pepperoni (or vice versa).

The implementation of each method in PizzaYourWay is simpler. However, you have made the user's job more difficult. This "slice before placing toppings" flow is now the caller's responsibility to code. They have to call five methods in the appropriate sequence in order to make a pizza.

The make() method in the SimplePizza may internally call private versions of mix_dough(), spin(), place_toppings(), bake(), and slice(). The make() method would handle any errors that these functions generated, thus simplifying the caller's code.

If you want to offer alternative flows, such as "slice before placing toppings," you could create another SimplePizza method such as make_by_slicing_before_placing_toppings(). The user simply calls the appropriate method, without having to deal with complexity. Now you are on the way to having a complete interface (see the previous section).

> ## Simplicity versus Complexity
>
> You always have trade-offs in life. The trade-off of "Simplicity, but Where?"* suggests you should strive for simplicity. You can make the API simpler, which will put more complexity (such as error handling) into the responsibility of the implementation, or you can make the implementation simpler, by adding complexity to the interface. This trade-off is also referred to as the "Law of Conservation of Complexity"†
>
> ---
> *David Bock suggested this name
> †Ron Thompson suggested this name

You could offer both interfaces to the outside world. The SimplePizza interface would call the appropriate methods in PizzaYourWay. In a sense, this trade-off acts as in reverse of the minimal versus complete. You create a simpler interface for a complex one.

SIMPLE

> Advantage—easy for the user to perform common functions

> Disadvantage—variations must be coded as new methods

COMPLEX

> Advantage—users have flexibility to "do it their way"

> Disadvantage—may be harder for users to understand

4.5 Things to Remember

Design cohesive interfaces. Determining what makes a cohesive interface is the hard part.

Aim for loose coupling. Using interfaces drives you there.

Measures of interfaces include the following:

- Minimal to complete

- Simple to complex

If in doubt, make an interface at one end of a measure, and use it from one made at the other end.

Chapter 5

Inheritance and Interfaces

Finding commonality among classes makes for effective object-oriented programming. Often, programmers express that commonality using an inheritance hierarchy, since that is one of the first concepts taught in object-oriented programming.

We're going to go to the other extreme in this chapter to explore the difference between using inheritance and using interfaces. An emphasis on interfaces guides you in determining what is the real essence of a class; once you have determined the essence, then you can look for commonalities between classes.

Creating an inheritance hierarchy prematurely can cause extra work when you then need to untangle it. If you start with interfaces and discover an appropriate hierarchy, you can easily refactor into that hierarchy. Refactoring into an inheritance hierarchy is far easier than refactoring out of an existing hierarchy.

We will look at examples of alternative designs that emphasize either inheritance or interfaces, so you can compare the two approaches. An interface-oriented alternative of a real-world Java inheritance hierarchy demonstrates the differences in code.

5.1   Inheritance and Interfaces

You probably learned inheritance as one of the initial features of object-oriented programming. With inheritance, a derived class receives the attributes and methods of a base class. The relationship between the derived and base class is referred to as "is-a" or more specifically as "is-a-kind-of." For example, a mammal "is-a-kind-of" animal. Inheritance creates a class hierarchy.

You may hear the term *inherits* applied to interfaces. For example, a PizzaShop that implements the PizzaOrdering interface is often said to inherit the interface.[1] However, it is a stretch to say that a PizzaShop "is-a" PizzaOrdering. Instead, a more applicable relationship is that a PizzaShop "provides-a" PizzaOrdering interface.[2] Often modules that implement PizzaOrdering interfaces are not even object-oriented. So in this book, we use the term *inherits* only when a derived class inherits from a base class, as with the **extends** keyword in Java. A class "implements" an interface if it has an implementation of every method in the interface. Java uses the **implements** keyword precisely for this concept.[3]

Inheritance is an important facet of object-oriented programming, but it can be misused.[4] Concentrating on the interfaces that classes provide, rather than on their hierarchies, can help prevent inheritance misuse, as well as yield a more fluid solution to a design. Let's look at some alternate ways to view example designs using both an inheritance-style approach and an interface-style approach. Both inheritance and interfaces provide polymorphism, a key feature of object-oriented design, so let's start there.

5.2 Polymorphism

A common form of polymorphism consists of multiple classes that all implement the same set of methods. Polymorphism of this type can be organized in two ways. With inheritance, a base class contains a set of methods, and derived classes have the same set of methods. The derived classes may inherit implementations of some methods and contain their own implementations of other methods. With interfaces, multiple classes each implement all the methods in the interface.

---

[1]Using a single term to represent two different concepts can be confusing. For example, how many different meanings are there for the keyword **static** in C++?

[2]You may see adjectives used for interface names, such as Printable;. With an adjective, you may see a reference such as a Document "is" Printable. The "is" in this case really means that a Document "provides-a" Printable interface.

[3]See the examples in Chapter 1 for how to code interfaces in C# and C++.

[4]See *Designing Reusable Classes* by Ralph E. Johnson and Brian Foote, http://www.laputan.org/drc/drc.html.

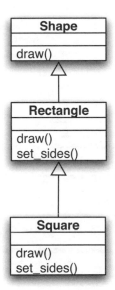

Figure 5.1: SHAPE HIERARCHY

With inheritance, the derived classes must obey the contract (of Design by Contract) of the base class. This makes an object of a derived class substitutable for an object of the base class. With interfaces, the implementation must also obey the contract, as stated in the First Law of Interfaces (see Chapter 2).

An example of an inheritance that violates a contract is the Shape hierarchy. The hierarchy looks like Figure 5.1.

```
class Shape
    draw()
class Rectangle extends Shape
    set_sides(side_one, side_two)
    draw()
class Square extends Rectangle
    set_sides(side_one, side_two)
    draw()
```

A Rectangle is a Shape. A Square is a Rectangle. Square inherits the set_sides() method from Rectangle. For a Rectangle, any two positive values for side_one and side_two are acceptable. A Square can accept only two equal values. According to Design by Contract, a derived class can have less strict preconditions and stricter postconditions. This

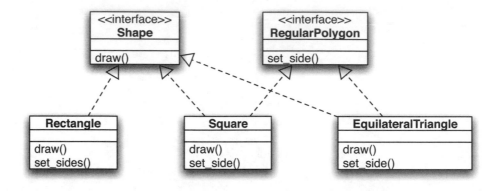

Figure 5.2: DIAGRAM OF INTERFACES

situation violates that rule, and thus the hierarchy is not ideal.

Although a Square is a Rectangle from a geometric point of view, it does not have the same behavior as a Rectangle. The error in this example comes from translating the common statement that "a square is a rectangle" into an inheritance hierarchy.

An alternative organization (Figure 5.2) using interfaces is as follows:

```
interface Shape
    draw()
Rectangle implements Shape
    set_sides(side_one, side_two)
    draw()
interface RegularPolygon
    set_side(measurement)
Square implements Shape, RegularPolygon
    set_side(measurement)
    draw()
EquilateralTriangle implements Shape, RegularPolygon
    set_side(measurement)
    draw()
```

With these interfaces, Square provides the Shape methods, but it also provides the methods in RegularPolygon. Square can obey the contract in both of these interfaces.

One difficulty with interfaces is that implementations may share common code for methods. You should not duplicate code; you have two ways to provide this common code. First, you can create a helper class and delegate operations to it. For example, if all RegularPolygons need to compute the perimeter and to compute the angles at the vertices, you could have this:

```
class RegularPolygonHelper
    set_side(measurement)
    compute_perimeter()
    compute_angle()
```

Implementers of RegularPolygon would delegate operations to this class in order to eliminate duplicate code.

Second, you could create a class that implemented the interface and provided code for many, if not all, of the methods (such as the Java Swing adapter classes for event listeners shown in Chapter 3). You would then derive from that class instead of implementing the interface. For example:

```
interface RegularPolygon
    set_side(measurement)
    compute_perimeter()
    compute_angle()
class DefaultRegularPolygon implements RegularPolygon
    set_side(measurement)
    compute_perimeter()
    compute_angle()
class Square extends DefaultRegularPolygon, implements Shape
    set_side(measurement)
    compute_perimeter()
    compute_angle()
    draw()
```

In the case of single-inheritance languages, you need to decide which of the two potential base classes (Shape or RegularPolygon) is the more important one. If you decide on Shape, then you'll still need RegularPolygonHelper. Determining which one is important can be difficult until you have more experience with the classes. Starting with interfaces allows your to postpone that decision until you have that experience.

USING INTERFACES
    Advantage—delay forming hierarchy until usage known

USING INHERITANCE
    Advantage—less delegation of common operations

5.3 Hierarchies

The animal kingdom is a frequently used hierarchy example. The hierarchy starts with Animal on top. Animal breaks down into Mammals,

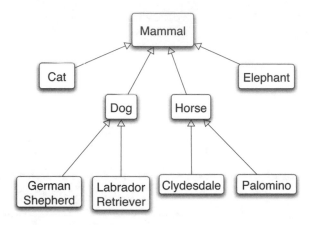

Figure 5.3: MAMMALIAN HIERARCHY

Fishes, Birds, Reptiles, Amphibians, etc. The relationships parallel those of an object-oriented hierarchy: a cow "is-a" Mammal. The subclasses (derived classes) have attributes in common with the superclasses (base classes). This zoological classification is based on characteristics used to identify animals; Figure 5.3 shows a portion of the standard hierarchy.

The animal hierarchy is useful for identification, but it does not necessarily represent behavior. The hierarchy represents data similarities. Mammals all have hair (except perhaps whales and dolphins), are warmblooded, and have mammary glands. The organization does not refer to services—things that animals do for us. Depending on your application that uses animals, a service-based description of animals may be more appropriate. The service-based description cuts across the normal hierarchy. Looking at what these animals do for us, we might have the following:

- Pull a Vehicle: Ox, Horse

- Give Milk: Cow

- Provide Companionship: Cat, Dog, Horse

- Race: Horse, Dog

- Carry Cargo: Horse, Elephant

- Entertain: Cat, Dog, Tiger, Lion, Elephant

Linnaean Taxonomy

Carolus Linnaeus developed the standard biological classification system. The system classifies species based on similarities in their forms and other traits that usually, but not always, reflect evolutionary relationships.

A problem with Linnaean taxonomy is that reclassification of an existing species or discovery of a new one can lead to changes in rank. Rank (i.e., in the Kingdom/Phylum/Class/Order/Family/Genus/Species breakdown) is denoted by suffices (e.g., "ae" as in "Hominidae"). A rank change requires renaming whole suites of taxonomic groups. (This need to reorganize an inheritance scheme may seem familiar to programmers.)

Phylocode is another biological classification system. It is based on common ancestry and the branching of the evolutionary tree. It is organized by species and clades—group of organisms sharing a particular ancestor. It is more immune to the need for reorganization. Just as in programming, picking the appropriate inheritance hierarchy can make changes simpler.*

*(See "Attacks on Taxonomy," *American Scientist*, July–August, 2005)

We could organize these methods in the same way we did printers in Chapter 3; e.g., each animal could have a "can you do this for me" method, such as can_you_carry_cargo(). Alternatively, we could have a set of interfaces as shown in Figure 5.4, on the next page. Animals would implement only the interfaces they could perform. The methods in the interfaces might be:

```
interface Pullers
    hook_up
    pull_hard
    pull_fast

interface MilkGivers
    give_milk
    give_chocolate_milk

interface CompanionshipGivers
    sit_in_lap
    play_for_fun
```

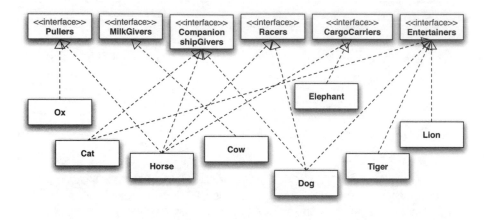

Figure 5.4: ANIMAL INTERFACES

```
interface Racers
    run_fast
    run_long

interface CargoCarriers
    load_up
    get_capacity

interface Entertainers
    jump_through_hoop
    stand_on_two_legs
```

Depending on the application, you may employ both a hierarchy and service-based interfaces. For example, you might have a Dog hierarchy whose base class implemented the methods for CompanionShipGivers, Racers, and Entertainers. Particular breeds of dogs could inherit from Dog to obtain a default implementation.

You might also have a need for interfaces based on common characteristics that cross hierarchies, such as LiveInWater, Vegetarian, etc. These interfaces could each have a helper class that provided common implementations. Classes such as Cow, Horse, and Ox could delegate to a VegetarianHelper class.

USING INTERFACES
    Advantage—can cross hierarchies

    Advantage—captures common attributes

Inheritance and Methods

Inheritance delineates a hierarchy of classes that all implement methods of the base class. The base class represents a general type, such as Mammal. The derived classes represent more specialized types, such as Cow and Horse. The derived classes may not necessarily offer additional methods.

On the other hand, derived classes can extend the base class and offer more methods. For example, for the Printer class in Chapter 4, a ColorPrinter represents more services than a Printer. When a derived class adds more methods to the base class, those additional methods can be considered an additional responsibility for the derived class. An interface could represent this additional responsibility.

For example, GUI components are usually organized as an inheritance hierarchy, like this:

```
class Component
    set_position()
    abstract draw()
class TextBox extends Component
    draw()
    set_text()
    get_text()
class CheckBox extends Component
    draw()
    set_state()
    get_state()
```

Here TextBox and CheckBox have additional methods that represent additional services for each derived class. Those additional methods could be denoted as interfaces, like this :

```
class Component
    set_position()
    abstract draw()
interface Textual
    set_text()
    get_text()
class TextBox extends Component, implements Textual
    draw()
    set_text()
    get_text()
```

```
interface Checkable
    set_state()
    get_state()
class CheckBox extends Component, implements Checkable
    draw()
    set_state()
    get_state()
```

If each derived class has its own unique set of additional methods, there is no advantage to organizing the hierarchy with interfaces. However, if many of the derived classes do have a common set of services, you may make those commonalities more apparent by using interfaces.

For example, a drop-down box and a multiple selection list are usually on one branch of a GUI hierarchy. Radio buttons and check boxes are on another branch of the hierarchy. These two separate branches are based on their relative appearances. Another way to group commonality is to put radio buttons and drop-down lists together and multiple-selections lists and check boxes together. Each of those groups has the same functionality. In the first group, the widgets provide selection of a single value. In the second group, the widgets provide the option of multiple values.[5] In this organization, they are grouped based on behavior, not on appearance. This grouping of behavior can be coded with interfaces:

```
interface SingleSelection
    get_selection()
    set_selection()
interface MultipleSelection
    get_selections()
    set_selections()
class RadioButtonGroup implements SingleSelection
class CheckBoxGroup implements MultipleSelection
class DropDownList implements SingleSelection
class MultipleSelectionList implements MultipleSelection
```

USING INTERFACES
      Advantage—can capture common set of usage

USING INHERITANCE
      Advantage—captures set of common behavior

---

[5]You might also put a list that allows only a single selection into this group.

Football Team

The members of a football team can be depicted with either inheritance or interfaces. If you represented the positions with inheritance, you might have an organization that looks like this:[6]

```
FootballPlayer
    run()

        DefensivePlayer extends Football Player
            tackle()

                DefensiveBackfieldPlayer extends DefensivePlayer
                    cover_pass()

        Offensive Player extends Football Player
            block()

                Center extends OffensivePlayer
                    snap()

                OffensiveReceiver extends OffensivePlayer
                    catch()
                    run_with_ball()

                OffensiveBackfieldPlayer extends OffensivePlayer
                    catch()
                    receive_handoff()
                    run_with_ball()

                Quarterback extends OffensivePlayer
                    handoff()
                    pass()
```

An object of one of these classes represents a player. So, Payton Manning would be an object of Quarterback. Based on the methods in the hierarchy, Payton can run, block, hand off, and pass. This hierarchy looks pretty good. On the other hand, we can make our organization more fluid by using interfaces, like this:

```
interface FootballPlayer
    run()
interface Blocker
    block()
interface PassReceiver
    catch()
```

---

[6]The services listed for each position are the required ones for each position. You could require that all FootballPlayers be able to catch and throw. The base class FootballPlayer would provide a basic implementation of these skills.

```
interface BallCarrier
    run_with_ball()
    receive_handoff()
interface Snapper
    snap()
interface Leader
    throw_pass()
    handoff()
    receive_snap()
interface PassDefender()
    cover_pass_receiver()
    break_up_pass()
    intercept_pass()
```

A *role* combines one or more interfaces. We might come up with the following roles for team members:

```
Center implements FootballPlayer, Blocker, Snapper
GuardTackle implement FootballPlayer, Blocker
EndTightOrSplit implements FootballPlayer, Blocker, PassReceiver
RunningBack implements FootballPlayer, BallCarrier, PassReceiver
Fullback implements Blocker, FootballPlayer, BallCarrier, PassReceiver
WideReceiver implements FootballPlayer, PassReceiver
Quarterback implements FootballPlayer, Leader, BallCarrier
```

Now along comes Deion Sanders, who plays both offense and defense. To fit Deion into the previous hierarchy, you need to create two objects: one an OffensivePlayer and the other a DefensivePlayer. Or you'd need to come up with some other workaround that does not fit cleanly into the hierarchy. With interfaces, Deion simply fulfills another role, like this:

```
SwitchPlayer implements FootballPlayer, PassReceiver, PassDefender
```

Roles can even be more fluid. For example, in one professional game, a backup quarterback lined up as a wide receiver.[7] Trying to fit such a role into a hierarchy can be daunting. With interfaces, he would have simply implemented PassReceiver, or he could take on a role like this:

```
ReceiverQuarterback implements FootballPlayer, PassReceiver, Quarterback
```

USING INTERFACES

Advantage—give more adaptability for roles that cross hierarchies

Disadvantage—may have duplicated code without helper classes to provide common functionality

---

[7]This was Seneca Wallace in a Carolina Panthers/Seattle Seahawks game, for you trivia buffs.

Using inheritance

Advantage—base classes can provide common implementations

Disadvantage—difficult to adapt to new situations.

5.4   An Interface Alternative for InputStream

What do football players, mammals, and geometric shapes have in common? We've used them as examples to show the differences between inheritance and interfaces. Let's look at a real-life class hierarchy and see how an alternative organization with interfaces would appear. This is a concrete example of the concepts discussed in the previous sections.

Java's java.io.InputStream class is an abstract class.[8] InputStream contains many methods defined as abstract, such as read(). Other methods are concrete but contain this statement in the documentation: "This method should be overridden by subclasses." A few other methods only suggest that they should be overridden. For example, a method that reads an array of bytes is provided. Its code simply calls the read() method for each byte, but the documentation suggests that a concrete implementation could code this better. Many methods in the class have an implementation that does nothing (e.g., close()).[9]

To contrast an inheritance approach with an interface approach in a real-code example, we will transform the InputStream hierarchy into an interface-based design. This transformation follows the concepts of the "Replace Inheritance with Delegation" refactoring.[10]

InputStream Interface

Suppose we have a CustomInputStream we developed by inheriting from InputStream such as in (Figure 5.5, on the following page. We start our transformation by extracting an interface from the current methods of the abstract InputStream class:

---

[8]See http://www.docjar.com/html/api/java/io/InputStream.java.html.

[9]This discussion ignores the additional methods that InputStream inherits from the Object. InputStream does not override any of those methods. Any implementation of the InputStream interface will also inherit from Object and thus have those same additional methods.

[10]See *Refactoring* by Martin Fowler, et al.

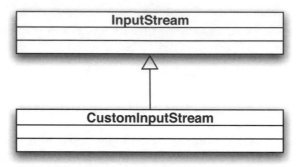

Figure 5.5: INHERITANCE

```
public interface InputStream
    {
    public int available() throws IOException;
    public void close()throws IOException;
    public void mark(int readlimit)
    public boolean markSupported()
    public int read()throws IOException;
    public int read(byte [] bytes) throws IOException;
    public int read(byte [] bytes, int offset, int length)
        throws IOException;
    public void reset()throws IOException;
    public  long skip(long n) throws IOException;
    }
```

The current implementation code in InputStream is put into a Input-
StreamDefault class as shown in Figure 5.6, on the next page. A particular InputStream, say CustomInputStream, inherits from InputStreamDefault:

```
public class InputStreamDefault implements InputStream
    {
    // same as current source of java.io.InputStream class
    }
public class CustomInputStream extends InputStream
    {
    }
```

At this point, we now have an interface that classes in other hierarchies can implement. We can transform CustomInputStream so that it
implements InputStream directly, by taking the method bodies in Input-
StreamDefault and moving them to CustomInputStream. But we would end
up with duplicate code if classes in other hierarchies implemented Input-
Stream. So, we remove the methods from InputStreamDefault and place

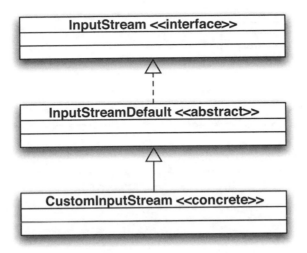

Figure 5.6: INHERITANCE

them in a helper class InputStreamHelper. CustomInputStream or other classes can delegate operations to this helper class. (See Figure 5.7, on the following page.)

```
public class InputStreamHelper
    {
    private InputStream inputStream;
    public InputStreamHelper(InputStream input)
        {
        inputStream = input;
        }
    public int read(byte [] bytes) throws IOException
        {
        read(byte[], 0, byte.length);
        }
    public int read(byte [] bytes, int offset, int length)
        throws IOException;
        {
        // calls inputStream.read() and places bytes into array
        }
    public long skip(long n) throws IOException
        {
        // Calls inputStream.read() to skip over n bytes
        }
    }
```

The code for CustomInputStream now looks like the following. We show details only for the methods where we delegate operations to the helper class.

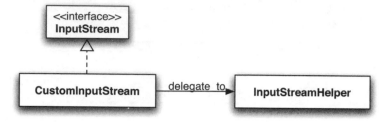

Figure 5.7: DELEGATION

```
class CustomInputStream implements InputStream
    {
    private InputStreamHelper inputHelper;
    public CustomInputStream()
        {
        inputHelper = new InputStreamHelper(this);
        }
    public int available() throws IOException {...}
    public void close()throws IOException {...}
    public void mark(int readlimit) {...}
    public boolean markSupported() {...}
    public int read()throws IOException {...}
    public int read(byte [] bytes) throws IOException
        {
        return inputHelper.read(bytes);
        }
    public int read(byte [] bytes, int offset, int length)
        throws IOException
        {
        return inputHelper.read(bytes, offset, length);
        }
    public void reset()throws IOException
    public long skip (long n) throws IOException
        {
        return inputHelper.skip(n) ;
        }
    }
```

The Input Marker

The mark methods (mark(), markSupported(), and reset()) in the java.io.
InputStream class are examples of "tell me if you do this" interfaces. For
those not familiar with the Java I/O library, these methods work as
follows.

If markSupported() returns true, then mark() can be used to mark a position in the input stream. When reset() is called, the next call to read() returns bytes starting at the marked position. So, the same bytes are returned again by read(). If the number of bytes read between the call to mark() and the call to reset() exceeds the readlimit number of bytes, then reset() does not have to work. Only classes that override markSupported() to return true need to implement mark() and reset().

If a method receives a reference to a java.io.InputStream object, it should call markSupported() before using mark() and reset().[11] The code for this method could look something like this:

```
void method(java.io.InputStream input)
    {
    if (input.markSupported())
        mark();
    //.... and other stuff
    }
```

The InputStream interface that we created includes the markSupported() method as well as the mark() and reset() methods. Instead of using the "can you do this" method approach, we can add another interface:

```
interface Markable
    {
    public void mark(int readlimit) ;
    public void reset()throws IOException ;
    }
```

Only classes that support mark() and reset() need to implement this interface. In a method, you can tell whether an InputStream supports marking by performing a cast. If an exception is thrown, you could pass the exception back to the caller as a violation of the interface contract. ("You must call this method with a Markable InputStream.") The code looks like this:

```
a_method(InputStream input) throws ClassCastException
    {
    Markable marking = (Markable) input;
    marking.mark();                    //...and  marking.reset()
    }
```

Alternatively, if the method can perform its operation in an alternative way without requiring the Markable interface, it does not need to throw the exception.

---

[11]I'm sure there is some application where calling mark() or reset() without checking markSupported() makes sense. I just can't think of one at the moment.

By separating the Markable interface, you're simplifying the InputStream interface. Also, it becomes clear from just looking at the class definition which classes support marking. For example:

```
class ByteArrayInputStream implements InputStream, Markable
```

This definitively shows you can mark an object of ByteArrayInputStream.[12]

FileInputStream: Yet Another Interface

We're still not done with evolving some more interfaces for InputStreams. The java.io.FileInputStream class is derived from the java.io.InputStream class. If we used interfaces as shown previously, we would state that FileInputStream implements InputStream and does not implement Markable. The java.io.FileInputStream class has additional methods that can be grouped as an interface, say FileInterface. This interface includes two methods:

```
FileInterface
    FileChannel getChannel()
    FileDescriptor getFD()
```

The java.io.FileDescriptor class refers to the underlying operating system file descriptor (equivalent to the Unix file descriptor shown in the Unix section in Chapter 1). The java.nio.channels.FileChannel class represents a way to asynchronously access a file.[13]

With FileInterface, FileInputStream can be described as follows:

```
class FileInputStream implements InputStream, FileInterface
```

java.io.FileOutputStream is the corresponding class for file output. It is derived from java.io.OutputStream in standard Java. Using interfaces, we could describe this class as follows:

```
class FileOutputStream implements OutputStream, FileInterface.
```

Note that FileInterface is implemented by both FileInputStream and FileOutputStream. This shows the relationship between these two classes that

---

[12]"Definitively" may be too strong a word. As one reviewer noted, "Just because you said you're going to do it, doesn't mean you really are doing it." Declaring the class to implement the interface really should imply that the class will honor the contract for the interface.

[13]FileChannel provides additional methods for reading and writing to a file. FileChannel is an abstract class that implements several interfaces. They include ByteChannel, Channel, GatheringByteChannel, InterruptibleChannel, ReadableByteChannel, ScatteringByteChannel, and WritableByteChannel. Without going into details about all these interfaces, suffice it to say that the structure of the channel classes reflects an interface-based approach to design.

appear on different branches in the standard Java hierarchy. With the standard library, there are separate implementations for the methods in each class. Seeing a common interface may prompt you to provide a common helper class for FileInterface that could eliminate this code duplication.

InputStream Review

When you have multiple implementations of an interface such as Input-Stream, you may duplicate logic in each implementation. If there are common implementation methods and you do not use a helper class, you may find yourself copying and pasting a lot. If you can create a well-defined hierarchy with many inheritable implementations, you are far better off using inheritance, rather than interfaces. But you may find that starting with interfaces and then refactoring to inheritance allows you to discover what is the best hierarchy.

INHERITANCE APPROACH

Advantage—easy to inherit an implementation

Disadvantage—may be difficult to adapt to changing roles

INTERFACE APPROACH

Advantages can be clearer what methods must be implemented.

A class in another inheritance hierarchy can provide the services of an interface.

Disadvantage—may end up with lots of helper classes.

5.5 Things to Remember

You can design with an emphasis on either inheritance or interfaces:

- Interfaces show commonality of behavior.

- Inheritance shows commonality of behavior along with commonality of implementation.

- Interfaces are more fluid than inheritance, but you need to use delegation to share common code.

- Inheritance couples the derived classes to the base class, but it allows them to easily share the common code of the base class.

Chapter 6

Remote Interfaces

Systems today are moving away from self-contained programs; they tend to interact with a number of other programs on remote hosts. Dealing with remote interfaces involves several more issues than does dealing with local interfaces, so we'll explore these facets now.

Many remote interfaces use a document style, rather than a procedural style. Document-style interfaces have a different paradigm from procedural-style interfaces and are less familiar to programmers, so we will investigate documents in some detail. We'll also examine how many of the concepts we discussed before are applicable to remote interfaces, such as statefulness versus statelessness.

6.1 Introduction

If you are physically in the pizza parlor, you can see the order taker. You are aware whether he is writing down your order or discussing last night's ball game with the cook. If you are local, you don't have to worry about failure to connect.

The pizza interface we introduced in the first chapter is really a remote interface: you make a connection over the phone network. Dealing with a remote interface is different from a local interface. A whole host of problems can occur that you might need to handle.

What if the phone is busy? Do you try the dialing again, or do you try another pizza parlor? Is the busy phone because of a failure in the phone company or a failure in the pizza parlor's phone?

What if it rings but no one answers? Do you try again, thinking you may have dialed the wrong number? Do you assume that they aren't open?

Suppose you get cut off in the middle of the call. Do you call back?

External Interfaces

The problems of pizza ordering exist in any external interface. An external interface is one called by other processes (either local or remote). External interfaces differ from local interfaces by network considerations, by nonhomogeneity of hosts, and by multiple process interactions.[1]

If an entire software system is contained within a single process, the system fails if the process fails. With a system consisting of multiple processes, a calling process (e.g., a client) has to handle the unavailability of other processes (e.g., a server). The client usually continues to run in spite of the failure of servers, but it needs either to communicate the server failure to the user or to act on that failure in a transparent manner, as per the Third Law of Interfaces.

Remote interfaces are external interfaces that are accessed over a network. In addition to server failure, with a network you may have a network delay or a network failure. Note that if you are unable to connect to a server, it is difficult to determine whether the network is down or whether the server is down. Likewise, a delay may be due to an overloaded network or an overloaded server that is handling too many clients. In either case, the client needs to handle the failure.

With nonhomogeneity, the client and the server may be different processor types (e.g., IBM mainframe versus PC). Even on a local machine, where processor types are not a consideration, the caller and server may be written in different programming languages.

Network Disruption

What would you do if you were ordering a pizza by phone and the call dropped before you heard how long it was going to take? You'd call back. You'd try to continue to describe the pizza you were ordering. But

---

[1]A local interface is usually called by only one process, although it may be called by multiple threads within that process. A remote interface can typically be concurrently called by multiple remote processes.

the pizza shop says, "I've had hundreds of orders in the last minute for just that type of pizza." You don't really want to order a second pizza. And the store owner doesn't want to make an unclaimed pizza. How would we change the pizza-ordering interface to avoid this?

The store owner could take some identification at the beginning of a call—a name or a phone number. If the circuit is broken, you call back and give the same name or phone number. If the order taker determines the name corresponds to one of the uncompleted orders, he pulls it off the shelf and resumes at the appropriate place in the order sequence.[2]

Getting initial identification is a form of planning for the possibility of communication disruption. The interface protocol should assume that the network may go down. In a manner similar to the pizza shop, interfaces can use client-generated IDs to ensure that service invocations are not duplicated. For example, when credit card transactions are submitted to a bank, the merchant identifies each transaction with a unique ID. If the connection is broken in the middle of transmitting a transaction, the merchant resubmits transactions that have not been explicitly confirmed. The bank knows by the ID for the particular merchant whether a transaction has already been posted. If the transaction has been posted, the bank merely confirms the transaction without reposting it.

6.2 Procedural and Document Interfaces

In our example in Chapter 1, you called the pizza shop over the phone. Your pizza shop may also accept fax orders. What is different about making a phone call versus sending a fax order? In either case, the order needs to be put into terms both you and the pizza shop understand. With the voice system, you execute a series of operations to create an order. With the fax, you have an order form that defines the required and optional data.

Problems are discovered immediately in the voice system. For example, you can ask for anchovies and get an immediate response. The voice on the other end can say "nope," meaning either they never have anchovies

---

[2]Some readers might note that a name such as Jim might be given for different orders. If the given name matches a previous name, the order taker may inform you that you have to give a different name. A phone number is not only good for identification but also for verification. The store owner can check the caller ID against the phone number to see whether it's the same one you said.

(a permanent error) or they don't have any today (a temporary error). In either case, you can make up your mind whether you want to have an anchovyless pizza or find some other pizza place.

With the a fax-based system, you fill out an order and await a response. The response may be a fax with the time till delivery or a fax saying, "Don't have any." If the latter, you need to alter your order and resubmit it. You may wonder whether your order was received. Since you may have to wait a while to get a fax back, it is harder to determine when to resend the order. The pizza parlor's fax may be out of paper. The scanner for the return fax may not be working. The order may have been put onto a pile. Only when the order is retrieved from the pile is a fax returned. We shall see how these issues of ordering by fax have parallels in remote interfaces.

External interfaces can use either procedural style or document style. A procedural interface looks like the interfaces we've been describing in this book. On the other hand, document-style interfaces use sets of data messages, similar to the fax-based pizza order.

For the most flexibility, the client (interface user) and the server (interface implementation provider) should be loosely coupled in terms of platform and language. A client written in any language should be able to access the server. You can accomplish this decoupling with either style.

Procedural Style

You can use Common Object Request Broker Architecture (CORBA) to define procedural-style interfaces that are both language and platform independent.[3] With CORBA, you specify the interface with the Interface Definition Language (IDL).[4] IDL looks a lot like a C++ header or a Java interface. A transformation program turns an IDL declaration into code stubs appropriate for a particular language and platform. An example of an interface defined in IDL is as follows:

```
enum Size {SMALL, MEDIUM, LARGE};
enum Toppings {PEPPERONI, MUSHROOMS, PEPPERS, SAUSAGE};
```

---

[3]You can define remote interfaces in a language-dependent manner, such as Java's Remote Method Invocation. You could also define them in a platform-dependent manner, such as Window's Distributed Component Object Model (DCOM).

[4]See http://www.omg.org for more information about CORBA and IDL.

```
interface PizzaOrdering
    {
    exception UnableToDeliver(string explanation);
    exception UnableToMake(string explanation);
    typedef Toppings ToppingArray[5];
    set_size(in Size the_size) raises (UnableToMake);
    set_toppings(ToppingArray toppings) raises (UnableToMake);
    set_address(in string street_address);
    TimePeriod get_time_till_delivered() raises (UnableToDeliver);
    }
```

Procedural-style remote interfaces look familiar to programmers. Calls to methods in remote interfaces (a Remote Procedure Call [RPC]) appear in your code as if they were calls to local interfaces. The only major difference is that the code must handle communication failure situations. RPCs are typically used for an immediate request/response in interactive situations. A client that called the PizzaOrdering interface can find out immediately whether the shop cannot make the pizza.

Procedural-style interfaces tend to be fine-grained. For example, they frequently contain operations for accessing individual values such as set_size() in the PizzaOrdering interface.

Document Style

With document style, the client and server interchange a series of data messages (documents). For a pizza order, the sequence might start with a document:

```
Document: PizzaOrder
    Size
    Toppings
    Address
```

The response could be either like this:

```
Document: SuccessResponse
    TimePeriod time_to_deliver
```

or like this:

```
Document: ErrorResponse
    String error_explanation
```

You may be less familiar with document-style interfaces. The documents represent a series of messages transmitted between the client and the service provider. The protocol is defined by the sequence of messages. We'll explore a typical sequence later in this chapter. Messages are not necessarily processed immediately. Response documents, such as SuccessResponse, may come almost immediately. However, they may also be delayed. A client using the document interface to order pizzas may not instantly find out whether the requested pizza can be made.

A document-style interface tends to be very coarse-grained. For example, a PizzaOrder document that contains the size and toppings is sent in a single operation, like this:[5]

```
interface Ordering
    submit_order(PizzaOrder)
```

PROCEDURAL STYLE

Advantage—remote and local interfaces can appear the same

Disadvantage—can require more communication (especially if fine-grained)

DOCUMENT STYLE

Advantage—can require less communication

Disadvantages—style is less familiar to programmers

6.3 Facets of External Interfaces

We discussed several facets of interfaces in Chapter 3. Now we'll examine some additional facets of external interfaces.

Synchronous versus Asynchronous

In Chapter 3, we described asynchronous event handling using the Observer pattern. Likewise, communication between a client and a server can be either synchronous or asynchronous. With synchronous interfaces, the client does not end communication until a result is returned.

With asynchronous interfaces, a result is returned at some other time after the client has ended the original communication. For example, documents are often placed on message queues. The client creates a

---

[5]The most general document interface consists of three operations:

Request/response—Document send_document_and_get_response(Document)

Request—void send_document(Document)

Response—Document receive_document()

That's so coarse-grained, you can transmit anything. (OK, maybe not anything, but almost anything).

document (message) and puts it onto a message queue. The client usually continues processing, handling other events. At some time, the server retrieves the message from the queue and processes the document. It then returns a response document, either directly to the client or back onto the queue for retrieval by the client.

Two typical combinations of modes for applications that use external interfaces are asynchronous/document (e.g., message queues) and synchronous/procedural (e.g., RPCs). You could consider the World Wide Web to be an synchronous/document interface: you send a document (e.g., a filled-in form) and receive a document (a new web page) in return. The least frequently used combination is asynchronous/procedural.

SYNCHRONOUS

    Advantage—practically immediate response

    Disadvantage—cannot scale up as well

ASYNCHRONOUS

    Advantage—can scale well, especially with document queues

    Disadvantage—documents should be validated on client before transmitting

Stateful versus Stateless

With remote interfaces, the distinction between stateful and stateless interfaces is more critical. A server that keeps state for clients may not be able to handle as many clients as a server that does not keep state.

For example, many web sites have shopping carts. In a stateful interface, the contents of the shopping cart are kept in a semipersistent storage on the server. Each new connection from a client (i.e., a browser) creates a new shopping cart that is assigned a SessionID. The SessionID is the key that identifies the data for a particular client on the server. The browser returns this SessionID with each request for another web page. The server uses the SessionID to retrieve current contents of the shopping cart.

In a stateless interface, the server does not keep any state. For example, with a Google search, the URL passes the search parameters every time. If Google keeps any information on a search, it is for performance reasons, rather than for interface reasons.

A stateful interface can be turned into a stateless interface in a manner similar to that shown in Chapter 3. All state information can be kept on the client and passed every time to the server. The server updates the state information and passes it back to the client. For a stateless shopping cart, the entire contents of the shopping cart are transmitted to and returned from the server for each web page.

REMOTE STATELESS

Advantages—servers can be easily scaled. If you have multiple servers processing client requests, any server can handle any client.

The service has redundancy. Any server could go down and the client could continue with any other server.

Disadvantage—amount of state information passed between client and server can grow, especially for a full shopping cart. In most cases, this amount will be less than the size of the web pages for which the state information is transferred.

REMOTE STATEFUL

Advantage—less information to communicate between client and server

Disadvantage—if using central database where the state information is stored, the amount of simultaneous connections to that database could be a limiting factor to scalability

Stability versus Flexibility

Stability is a needed trait for external interfaces. You typically have no knowledge of who is accessing the interface, so you can't change it willy-nilly. However, flexibility is also needed for interfaces, since you may want to add features to them in the future. Both procedural and document interfaces can be flexible.

You should follow a few guidelines in being flexible in interfaces. First, never alter the semantics of existing methods or data. Second, you can add methods or data; just don't expect that users will add calls to the new methods or provide the new data. For example, you could add a country field to an address. But you still should handle a document that does not contain a country, by creating a reasonable default value for country.

But although adding functionality is easy, deleting methods or data is hard. Callers may still expect that they still exist and call the methods or supply the data. Methods in some computer language libraries that have been designated as "deprecated" may still be called years later. Only if you have control of both sides of the interface (the client and the server), or you have a sufficiently desired interface, do you have a possibility of deleting deprecated methods.[6]

All interfaces should be identified by an explicit version ID. An ID provides a simpler way to determine the version of the client than by ascertaining which particular methods or data a client uses. Knowing a client's version aids the server in dealing with older versions. A server should be able to handle not only the current version of a service but also older versions. Obviously at some point, you would like to be able to remove support for really old versions. Depending on the importance of your service to the clients and your relative political strength, you may need to continue to handle numerous versions for a long time.[7]

6.4 Discovery of Services

You've come to a new city. You're dying for a pizza. You look up in the Yellow Pages[8] for a pizza place. (Ok, maybe you look on Google Maps to find a close one.) You look under *Pizza*. You know that any listed pizza shop should implement the PizzaOrdering interface.[9] How do you pick one from the hundreds of pizza places listed? You can choose the random method, the first on the list, the closest, or you can go for a known brand name.

You probably did this lookup once in your hometown and posted the phone number on your bulletin board. That parallels how Microsoft's DCOM works. You make an entry in the registry to indicate where a

---

[6]The situation of telling users that methods that have been marked as deprecated are finally being deleted is similar to that of passengers boarding a plane. Even though all the passengers know when the flight is leaving, some passengers still need to be informed over the loudspeakers. Even then, the gate agent needs to decide when to finally let the plane depart without the missing passengers.

[7]To help you determine when it's appropriate to remove support, you can log the version IDs that clients use to access an interface. When the log shows that the only clients using the old version are those for whom you have blackmailable information, you can remove the old version.

[8]It's always amazing what you learn when writing a book: "Yellow Pages" is a trademark in the public domain.

[9]How do you know it's really a pizza shop? Maybe the pizza is made on a truck as it's on its way to deliver the pizza to you.

Versioning

Versioning of interfaces is an old problem. Microsoft Windows spawned the condition known as "DLL hell" in which incompatible versions of the same interface implementations (e.g., in dynamic link libraries) were needed by different programs on the same computer. In the .NET Framework Microsoft has solved this problem by creating versioned assemblies.

The same versioning issue occurs with JAR files. The Java Community Process is developing the Java Module System (JSR-277).* JMS "defines a distribution format and a repository for collections of Java code and related resources." One of its components is a "versioning scheme that defines how a module declares its own version as well its versioned dependencies upon other modules."

---

*See `http://www.jcp.org/en/jsr/detail?id=277`. David Bock, a member of the committee, suggested this example.

---

particular interface is implemented. Later, you bypass the directory service when getting the service.

We show in Chapter 9 a general directory mechanism for services. Directory services of frameworks such as CORBA and web services work similar to the one shown in that chapter. Similar to you using the Yellow Pages for finding a pizza place, a service consumer (e.g., a client) can use the directory service to discover the identity of service providers (e.g., a server) for a particular service. In addition, the directories can provide the communication protocol and other information needed to communicate with a service.

The consumer may be able to choose between providers (e.g., from which host to download an open source software package). Alternatively, the directory service can select one, based on some type of algorithm (round robin, who is the cheapest, etc.). This automatic selection of a server is often used when your browser requests a web server (one that implements the Hypertext Transfer Protocol [HTTP] interface) for a particular domain. The directory server returns the address of one of a number of servers, making the multiplicity of servers opaque to the client.

<hr>

Published versus Unpublished _____

You can easily redesign interfaces used only within a program. You only have that program to worry about. Restructuring or refactoring the code to make the internal interfaces more consistent, more cohesive, and less coupled is always beneficial.

Interfaces that are used by multiple systems or development groups are more challenging. An interface used by multiple systems can be considered "published." Martin Fowler suggests delaying publishing interfaces since they cannot easily be changed. Once they're published, you have to worry about all the users of the interface.*

For intracorporate interfaces, an individual or committee could be responsible for the coordination of publishing interfaces, especially for interfaces that are planned as utility interfaces for the enterprise. The coordinators look at the interface from the user's side. For example, they may check to see that its style matches those of existing interfaces and the protocol is logical. Examples of enterprise interfaces are a user authentication interface for single logon and a universal logging capability for applications.

_____

*Cf. http://www.martinfowler.com/ieeeSoftware/published.pdf.

6.5 More on Document Style

Since using documents as interfaces may be less familiar to many developers, we continue our exploration of some of the facets of this style.

Document Representation

You can represent documents in either external format or internal format. Common external formats are XML, EDI, and ANSI X12. In most languages, a pure data object, such as a DTO, can represent the internal format of a document. Most documents have tree-like structures, which DTOs can parallel. To keep the external representation opaque, modules (other than those that actually convert the data to and from external format) should deal with the DTO, rather than with the external form.

Suppose we decided to use XML as the external format for the PizzaOrder shown earlier in this chapter:

```
<Pizza>
    <Size>Large</Size>
    <Toppings>
        <Topping>Pepperoni</Topping>
        <Topping>Mushroom</Topping>
    </Toppings>
    <Address>
        <Street>1 Oak Street</Street>
        <City>Mytown</City>
    </Address>
</Pizza>
```

We can create an internal representation of this document:

```
class PizzaOrder
    set_size(Size)
    set_topping(Topping)
    Size get_size()
    Topping [] get_toppings()
    set_size(Address)
    Address get_size()
```

Only when we send a PizzaOrder to an external interface do we need to convert the data to and from an external from, such as XML:[10]

Validating a Document

Did what you wrote on the order make sense to the pizza parlor staff? Is the information readable? Based on an order that passes a validity check, can the pizza parlor process the order? Does it have all the necessary ingredients?

Like procedural interfaces, documents have interface contracts. There are multiple levels of validity checking for a document to ensure that it meets the interface contract: the syntax of the text itself, constraints on the values, and validity of the values.[11] Before sending a document, you should validate the data and check the constraints as thoroughly as possible to avoid needless retransmission.

---

[10]If the document is large and converting the entire document is resource intensive, you can deal with it in an iterative form, such as SAX (shown in Chapter 3).

[11]A procedural-style interface has fewer levels of validity checking, since the syntax is checked by the compiler and some constraints can be specified by using specific data types for method parameters.

Suppose we represent the data in an XML format. The XML data must be well-formed (e.g., the tags are correctly formed with nested begin/end tags, etc.). An XML schema describes the required and optional fields in an XML document. The organization of XML data should be valid; that is, it should conform to a particular schema.[12]

Values of each of the data items have constraints that need to be honored, such as the type of data and low and high limits. An XML schema not only can outline the structure of XML data; it can also give constraints on the data.

Some data constraints are expressible in a schema, and some are not. For example, the schema can require that a data item must be one of a set of choices or that a date must be in a particular range (the order must be placed today or in the future). However, cross-data constraints are difficult to express in a schema. For example, if you order beer in a pizza parlor, then you have to order a pizza.[13]

You might perform validity checks by using an XML tool or by transforming the document into a DTO and performing the checks in another language. If you use a DTO to represent a document, you can perform many of the validity checks in the set methods. You can also easily perform cross-value checks, as well as any other rules that are not expressible in a schema.

You can perform many data checks on the client computer. For example, the client can check a CustomerID for the number and types of characters. There are other checks that only the server can perform. For example, is a CustomerID one that is registered in the system? Some other checks might be difficult for both systems (the client or the server) to perform, such as whether the sender of a document legally represents a particular customer.

Document Encoding

Although XML is a very adaptable and general form of encoding documents, it is not the only one. Depending on the environment in which the document is used, you might find other encodings more efficient.

---

[12]Creating a valid, well-formed XML document is a relatively simple task with modern tools. (See http://www.w3.org/TR/xmlschema-0/ for more information about schemas.)

[13]This is a law in at least one town in Massachusetts.

Here are several alternative text encodings, along with examples of where they are employed:

- Straight text (text with line breaks is a lingua franca). Examples:
    - Email messages
    - Pipes and filters of Unix
- Text with field delimiters. Examples:
    - Email headers
    - Comma or tab delimited files
- Text with named tokens. Examples:
    - Property files[14]
    - HTTP form parameters
- Structured text, e.g., XML and YAML.[15] Examples:
    - Web services
    - Configuration files
- Electronic Document Interchange (EDI) standards. Examples:
    - Airline reservation systems
    - Electronic orders[16]

Your application may require you to use a particular format for communication. If not, select the simplest representation. XML is a good choice for complex documents because of the number of tools available for manipulating that format. However, if all you require is a few values, using named tokens can be simpler.

Document-Based Business Flow

Similar to protocols for calling methods for a procedure-style interface, there are protocols for document-style interfaces. You can't send a series of documents in just any order. The order must correspond to a business flow.

---

[14]The old-style Microsoft Windows .ini files are an example of a property file.
[15]See www.yaml.org.
[16]See "Using Standard Documents" in the appendix.

Let's look at something that you may often do on the Web and see how this flow is represented as an exchange of documents.[17] These documents correspond to data sent from forms in your browser and data returned on the displayed web pages. The encoding in one direction is named tokens, and the encoding in the other direction is structured text (Hypertext Markup Language [HTML]).

You go to Orbitz, Travelocity, or another travel site. You enter a request for a one-way airfare from your home to New York City and click Search. The transmitted information can be considered a *request for quotation* document. The web browser transmits this information in the form of tokens in the HTTP request:

```
Document: RequestForQuotationForOneWayAirfare
    Origin
    Destination
    Date
    Number Travelers
```

The response to this document is another document:[18]

```
Document: QuotationForOneWayAirfare
    Selections []
        FareAllInclusive
        Legs []
            Flight Number
            Origin
            Destination
            DateTime Departure
            DateTime Arrival
```

Once you have made your choice of the selections, you send back another document:

```
Document: ReserveOneWayAirfare
    Passenger
    FareAllInclusive
    Legs []
        Flight
        Number
        Origin
        Destination
        DateTime Departure
        DateTime Arrival
```

---

[17]To see another example, check out the Oasis Universal Business Language (UBL) 1.0, published September 15, 2004. (ID: cd-UBL-1.0). You can find a copy at http://docs.oasis-open.org/ubl/cd-UBL-1.0/.

[18]And perhaps a call from the Department of Homeland Security; one-way flights seem to get them a little skittish.

The contents of ReserveOneWayAirfare could be shorter, if the server were stateful. The server would need to remember what Selections had been transmitted. Then ReserveOneWayAirfare could contain just an index into the Selections of the QuotationForOneWayAirfare document. Once the travel site has confirmed your reservation, the site returns a confirmation document:

```
Document: ReservationConfirmation
    Reservation Identification
    Passenger
    FareAllInclusive
    Legs []
        Flight Number
        Origin Destination
        DateTime Departure
        DateTime Arrival
```

In the next step you pay for the reservation with the following document:

```
Document: Payment
        Reservation Identification
        Credit Card Number
        Credit Card Information
        Amount
```

And the system returns this:

```
Document: PaymentReceived
        Reservation Identification
```

The preceding documents communicate information between your web browser and the web server. On the web server side, processing these documents may generate other documents, such as requests for quotations to the individual reservation systems for each airline, and charge documents to a credit card processor.

Many other conditions may exist for this document sequence. For example, you may have temporal constraints. If the Payment document is not received within a given period of time after ReservationConfirmation is sent, the reservation may be canceled.

A document flow can be expressed in procedural code. Assume each of the documents has been transformed into a corresponding DTO. You could code the sequence shown in Figure 6.1, on the next page as follows:

```
RequestForQuotationForOneWayAirfare rfq;
    // Fill in rfq with desired values, then
QuotationForOneWayAirfare quotation = send_message(rfq)
```

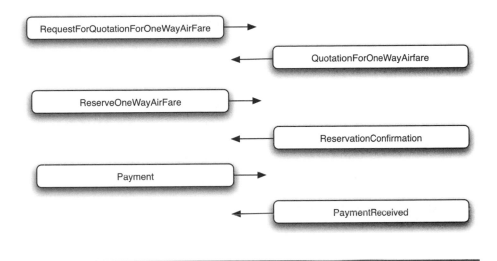

Figure 6.1: DOCUMENT FLOW

```
    // Put up GUI with selection
ReserveOneWayAirfare reserve;
    // When user has selected an item, fill in reserve
    // and send it
ReservationConfirmation confirmation = send_message(reserve)
Payment payment;
    // Fill in payment with amount and other information
PaymentReceived payment_received = send_message(payment)
```

6.6 Security

Whenever you have an remote interface that is available to the outside world, you need to worry about security. A detailed examination of security topics is beyond the scope of this book, so we'll just discuss some general matters.[19] Frameworks such as web services and CORBA provide some solutions to general security issues such as authentication and confidentiality. However, you should examine each remote interface to ensure that it is secure.

You need to authenticate the user of your interface. Authentication determines, to a reasonable degree of certainty, that the user is really

---

[19]See *Software Security: Building Security In* by Gary McGraw (Addison-Wesley Professional, 2006) for a full discussion of security.

the user. Typical authentication schemes range from passwords to encrypted certificates to biometric scans.

Once you know who the user is, you should check to see that the user is authorized to access the interface or perform an operation. Typically, authorization is performed using an access control list (ACL) or similar mechanism. The ACL lists the users who are authorized to perform a particular operation. To simplify administration, users are often assigned roles, such as Customer or PizzaOrderer. The ACL associates roles with particular operations or set of operations.

When data is transmitted over a network, you particularly need to be concerned with confidentiality and data integrity. Encrypting data can provide a degree of confidentiality. It can help prevent the data from being altered as it traverses the network.

Even if you have mechanisms for providing all the previously mentioned security aspects, you need to worry about information escaping. Suppose you work for a hospital and you use a remote provider to check the ZIP codes for addresses. If those addresses are your patients' addresses, you just provided private patient data to an unauthorized party.

You should be particularly concerned with contract checking. Any document-style interface should completely check the validity of the received documents. Implementations of procedural-style interfaces should employ strong contract checking, since the implementations cannot be assured that the client has followed the contract.

6.7 Testing

In general, every external interface should have a testing implementation (e.g., a stub or a mock object). The testing implementation can respond quicker than a remote implementation. The quick response improves the speed of testing other units that depend on the remote interface. The testing implementation can have additional methods (a testing interface) that allow the user to set up a desired request/response scenario (e.g., a request document and a response document). It can also provide a way to create a failure condition (e.g., server unavailable) to see how the unit under test handles those conditions. Simulating these failures in software for rapid testing is a lot easier than having to disconnect the network.

6.8 Things to Remember

We covered both procedural-style and document-style remote interfaces. When using or designing a remote interface, consider how it may react to network delay or failure and make provisions for handling those situations. For a document-style interface, follow these tips:

- Precisely specify the document flow protocol.

- Perform validity checking before transmitting a document.

- Use an appropriate document encoding schema.

We discussed a few matters that you should consider when you employ a remote interface:

- Use a DTO or a data interface to make the external representation of a document more opaque.

- Examine the security implications of any remote interface.

Part II

Developing with Interfaces

Chapter 7

A Little Process

You probably already have a software development process. You may be using the Rational Unified Process (RUP) or Extreme Programming (XP) or something in between. This chapter shows how interface-oriented design can fit into your process; we'll outline the development phases for a system with a concentration on interfaces. In the next three chapters, we will create three types of systems to show interfaces at work in other contexts.

Creating interfaces may seem contrary to a common measure of simplicity, which is having the fewest lines of code. Using interfaces can add code. However, designing with interfaces focuses on creating a contract for an interface and testing that contract. It can prevent you from getting mired in implementation details too early. Even if you decide not to have the interface layer in code, thinking in interfaces helps keep you focused on the real problems. Since refactoring consists of changing code without changing its external interface, a well-designed interface can make it easier to refactor.

7.1 The Agile Model

Since I do agile development in my work, I present interface-oriented design in that context. We are not going to cover the details of agile development methodologies. You can read these details in various books on agile processes.[1]

---

[1] Books include *Extreme Programming Explained: Embrace Change* by Kent Beck and Cynthia Andres (Addison-Wesley, 2004), or *Agile Software Development with SCRUM* by Ken Schwaber and Mike Beedle (Prentice Hall, 2001).

In agile development, you create your software in iterations. During each iteration, you create the highest-priority remaining features desired by the customer. This chapter shows discrete tasks of development—vision, conceptualization, testing, analysis, design, and implementation. During an iteration, you may go through all these tasks to develop a feature.

I outline specific development tasks to be able to separate the discussion of the various portions of the process; no absolute milestones signal the end of one phase and the beginning of another. And these phases aren't followed linearly—feedback exists among them. You may discover during implementation that an ambiguity existed in conceptualization. You would go briefly back to conceptualizing, disambiguate the concept, and then continue implementing.

7.2 Vision

Every software project needs a vision. The vision is a sentence or two that outlines the business purpose for the software. In this chapter as an example, we are going to create a pizza shop automator. The vision is that this system decreases the amount of work necessary to process pizza orders.

7.3 Conceptualization

Once you've established a vision, you need to capture requirements for the software system. Functional requirements can be expressed in many ways including formal requirement documents, user stories, and use cases. I have found that use cases are easy for both the end user and the developer to understand. They quickly demonstrate what the system does for the user, as well as show what is inside the system and outside the system. They form the basis for acceptance tests as well as for internal interface tests. If a system cannot perform what the use cases state, then the system has failed.[2]

We create the use cases together with the person requesting the system and the end users. For the pizza shop automator, the actual making

---

[2]Passing tests for the use cases is necessary for system success but not sufficient. The system must also pass nonfunctional tests (e.g., performance, robustness).

Joe Asks...
Use Cases

A use case* "defines the interactions between external actors and the system under consideration to accomplish a business goal. Actors are parties outside the system that interact with the system; an actor can be a class of users, a role that users can play, or another system."

Use cases treat the system as a "black box." Interactions with the system, including system responses, are documented from outside the system. This is deliberate policy, because it simplifies the description of requirements and avoids the trap of making assumptions about how this functionality will be accomplished.

Note that this definition parallels how interfaces should be treated.

Each use case has a name, shown in the use case diagram. For each use case, you write down the individual steps that list what the user does and how the system responds. A simple format is as follows:†

 Use Case: Title

   1. User asks.

   2. System responds

---

*This definition comes from `http://en.wikipedia.org/wiki/Use_cases`.
†You can add many more features to use cases. See *Writing Effective Use Cases* by Alistair Cockburn (Addison-Wesley Professional, 2000) for details.

---

the pizza and delivering the pizza are outside of the software system.[3] For this system, the main concern is the information flow between the various actors.

We first identify the actors by the roles that they play, not their specific

---

[3]If we were creating an automated pizza shop, then the making of the pizza would be inside the system.

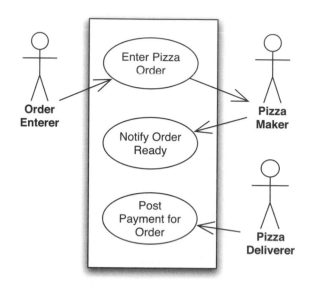

Figure 7.1: USE CASES

positions. An OrderEnterer could be the person on the other end of the phone, or it could be a customer on a web site. A PizzaDeliverer could be a guy in a car, or it could be someone behind the counter who delivers the pizza to a walk-in customer. We next determine what the actors will use the system for and list these in a use case diagram (Figure 7.1).

For each use case, we list the interactions between the user and the system. We try to write the interactions in a more general way (e.g., select the size of pizza), rather than in a specific way (e.g., choose the size of pizza from a drop-down list).[4] We want to explore the functionality of the user interface, rather than a specific implementation at this point. Here are the details for each use case:

 Use Case: Enter Pizza Order

1. Order Enterer enters order details.

2. System responds with time period till order is to be delivered.

---

[4]You can create GUI prototypes that use specific widgets, if the user needs to envision how the system will appear to the end user in order to understand it.

Use Case: Notify Order Ready

1. Pizza Maker notifies system that order is complete.

2. System notifies Pizza Deliverer that order is ready for delivery.

Use Case: Post Payment for Order

1. Pizza Deliverer enters payment received from customer.

2. System records order as paid.

3. Pizza Deliverer puts remainder of money into his pocket as tip.

Each use case represents a portion of the user's interface to the system. Like the code-based interfaces we have been discussing, the user's interface has a contract and a protocol. We can also document the preconditions and postconditions for each use case. For example, "Notify Order Ready" has a precondition that "Enter Pizza Order" has occurred.

Before moving onward, it's a good idea to write down some of the assumptions we are making for this system. We simplified the flow to concentrate on the process. We know that one pizza is just not enough for a hungry customer. Our assumptions include the following:

- An order is for one pizza and no other menu items. Otherwise, we need to handle partial orders (e.g., one pizza is ready, and another is not).

- The system will handle only cash payments for pizza.

- Pizzas vary only by size and number of toppings.

Testing

It may seem odd to mention testing before even starting to design the system, but outlining tests can provide additional insights in understanding a system. Often, you can find ways to structure your interfaces to make them easier to test. On the user level, we examine the use cases to create an outline of the acceptance tests. Here are some tests that we generated from the use cases:

Test Case: Normal Pizza Order

1. Order Enterer enters Pizza order.

2. Order Enterer should see time to deliver.

3. Pizza Maker should see order.

4. Pizza Maker notifies order is complete.

5. Pizza Deliverer should see delivery notice.

6. Pizza Deliverer enters payment from customer.

7. System should show order is paid.

Test Case: Normal Pizza Orders

1. Repeat Normal Pizza Order several times.

2. System should show all orders are paid for.

Test Case: Random Pizza Payments

1. Like Normal Pizza Orders, but Pizza Deliverer pays for orders in random sequence.

2. System should show all orders are paid for.

These tests suggest that we should have a reporting mechanism that lists orders and whether they have been paid. We can use that reporting mechanism to determine the success of these tests. This reporting mechanism suggests that we didn't capture a use case involving reports.

You can also generate "misuse" cases, which describe how the system might be accidentally or deliberately misused. Misuse cases can include the "fringe" cases in which you try entering values that are on the edge of an acceptable range. Here are a few misuse cases:

Test Case: Pay for Paid Order

1. Pizza Deliverer pays for order that has already been paid.

2. System should not allow this.

Test Case: Overburden Pizza Maker

1. Order Enterer enters numerous orders for same address.[5]

---

[5]The same address is used in order to differentiate the response from that due to delivery to different addresses.

2. System should respond with increasing time to deliver.

Test Case: Send Pizza Deliverer on Goose Chase

1. Order Enterer enters order for faraway place.

2. System should respond with what?

The third test suggests that we have not yet captured some requirements, since we are not sure how the system should respond. Our users inform us that a pizza shop has a limited delivery area to ensure that the delivered pizza is hot. You should not accept an order if the delivery address is outside that delivery area. The idea of addresses inspires a few more misuse cases:

Test Case: Place Order to Nonexistent Address

1. Order Enterer places order to nonexistent address.

2. System should respond that it cannot deliver to that address.

Test Case: Make Them Run All Over the Place

1. Order Enterer places orders to address that are widely separated and timed so that they cannot all be delivered together.

2. System should respond that delivery time will be excessive.

These cases revolve around a common theme: the system should be able to determine the validity of an address and to determine the delivery time for a particular address. We already know of some implementations that perform these operations (e.g., maps.google.com and mapquest.com). When we get around to creating this feature, we'll create an interface that makes transparent which implementation we are using.

We can come up with other misuse cases that test how the system responds to large demands:

Test Case: Make Them Run Out of Ingredients

1. Order Enterer orders many, many pizzas.

2. System at some point should respond that it cannot handle any more.

This "Denial of Pizza" attack is the equivalent of a "Denial of Service" network attack. Keep pounding at something to see whether it gives up. The first release may not be able to pass this test, but we'll keep it on the list for future releases.

We could make up many more misuse cases, but you should get the point by now. Each of these misuse cases helps us define the contract for the user interface—how the system should respond for each operation that the user requests.

7.4 Analysis and Design

The real boundary between analysis and design is not precise, but you can separate them with formal definitions. *Analysis* is the process of identifying the essential concepts (abstractions) in a system and determining the work that needs to be performed. *Design* develops those abstractions into realizable components. In implementation, you write the code for those components. In reality, you may develop some concepts and implement them and then realize that you did not completely understand the concept.

The term *design* is often applied to both analysis and design. The title of this book is *Interface-Oriented Design* (IOD). The ideas of IOD appear both in developing the abstractions and in turning those abstractions into components.

7.5 Interface-Oriented Design

Interface-oriented design encompasses ideas found in other design philosophies as responsibility-driven design, role-based design, and test-first development.

Interface-oriented design revolves around these concepts:

- An interface represents a set of responsibilities.

- A responsibility is a service that the interface provides.

- Modules implement interfaces. A module can be a class, a component, a remote service, or even a human being performing operations manually.

- A role represents one or more related interfaces.

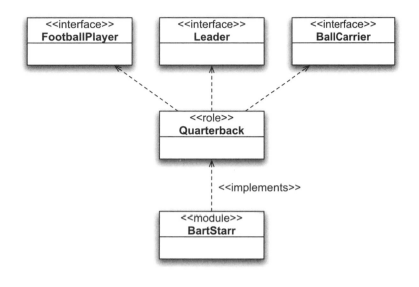

Figure 7.2: INTERFACES, ROLES, AND MODULES

- A module can implement one or more interfaces so that it can play a role or multiple roles.

The diagram in Figure 7.2, shows the relationship between interfaces, roles, and implementations. The interfaces and roles are the ones described in Chapter 5. Bart Starr is an implementation of the Quarterback role.[6]

In analysis, interface responsibilities are expressed in general terms. In design, these responsibilities are usually expressed as methods. Some responsibilities assigned to an interface may not be exposed as a method, but simply end up as internal operations. In analysis, you can come up with a rough draft of the interfaces for a system. You then assign responsibilities to those interfaces. Alternatively, you can start by grouping responsibilities into sets (roles) and then assigning names to those roles.

Once you've come up with a draft of the interfaces and their responsibilities, you work your way through the use cases to see whether they can be performed with those interfaces.

---

[6]Bart Starr was the quarterback for the Green Bay Packers and MVP of Super Bowls I and II.

How do you determine which interface is assigned which responsibility? Here are a few general guidelines:

- Put together cohesive interfaces. The responsibilities should be ones that seem like they go together.

- Decouple interfaces—separate responsibilities that may be implemented differently.

- Divide into more interfaces to simplify the testing of each interface.[7]

Rebecca Wirfs-Brock in *Responsibility Driven Design*[8] suggests a number of stereotypes for objects. A stereotype describes the general category of use for an object. Those stereotypes have a correspondence in interface-oriented design. We already listed two (data interface and service interface) in Chapter 2. Other stereotypes include the following:

- Storage interfaces (to hold persistent data)

- Entity interfaces that reflect models and business rules

- Interfaces to outside world
  - Document interfaces
  - View/controller GUI interface

No guaranteed way exists to determine what responsibilities should go with which interfaces; designing interfaces takes the same effort as designing classes. Bertrand Meyer says, "Finding classes is the central decision in building an object-oriented software system; as in any creative discipline, making such decisions right takes talent and experience, not to mention luck." He goes on to say, "No book advice can replace your know-how and ingenuity." The same can be said for finding the right set of cohesive interfaces.

IRI Cards

For analysis, I like to use what I call *IRI cards*, which are a variation of the CRC cards of Ward Cunningham, Kent Beck, and Rebecca Wirfs-Brock. CRC stands for class-responsibility-collaboration. IRI stands

---

[7]If you find yourself winding up with most interfaces having a single method, then you are probably breaking up cohesive responsibilities.

[8]See *Object Design: Roles, Responsibilities, and Collaborations* by Rebecca Wirfs-Brock and Alan McKean (Addison-Wesley Professional, 2002).

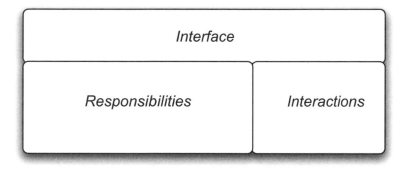

Figure 7.3: IRI CARD TEMPLATE

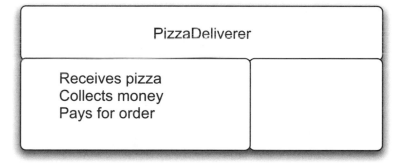

Figure 7.4: IRI CARD EXAMPLE

for interface-responsibility-interaction. A IRI template is shown in Figure 7.3. The main difference is that emphasizing interfaces makes the cards more useful in designing both class- and service-oriented designs, and it removes some emphasis on implementation issues, such as classes.

On an index card, write down an interface name and a set of responsibilities. Continue until all responsibilities are assigned to an interface.

If the responsibilities are complex, break them down into simpler ones.

Typically these simpler responsibilities will be offered by other interfaces. Create another card with names for those additional interfaces and the responsibilities. Those additional interfaces are listed as interactions on the interface card that needs them.

It's not always necessary to go from the top down (starting from the exterior responsibilities that are large and going inward to the most detailed interface). You can start at either place. Starting at the bottom may point out more reusable interfaces.

Examining our use cases, we come up with a preliminary set of interfaces. We could show these on index cards, such as the example shown in Figure 7.4, on the page before, but that would just take up more room. I tend to create more interfaces in the beginning. I have found it's easier to combine responsibilities from two or more cohesive interfaces and then separate an interface's responsibilities into multiple interfaces.

- Interface Pizza
  - Keep track of size and kinds of toppings
- Interface Address
  - Keep track of street, city, ZIP, phone number
  - Determine distance to another address
- Interface Order
  - Contains Pizza and Address
- Interface OrderEnterer
  - Enter pizza order
  - Display time to deliver
- Interface PizzaMaker
  - Display pizza order to create
  - Notify when order is ready
- Interface PizzaDeliverer
  - Receives pizza
  - Collects money
  - Pays for order

Now that we have a preliminary set of interfaces, we start with the use cases and see whether we have captured all the responsibilities. Let's take the first use case, which we restate with the interfaces we have created:

Use Case: Normal Pizza Order

1. OrderEnterer enters Pizza order.

2. OrderEnterer should see time to deliver.

Between the OrderEnterer, Order, and Pizza, we think that we have captured all the responsibilities for this use case, but we need to check. So we trace how the system determines the time till an order is ready. The OrderEnterer asks the PizzaMaker how long it will take to complete the order. Then the OrderEnterer asks the PizzaDeliverer how long it will take to deliver the pizza, assuming it is ready when the PizzaMaker says it will be. Then the system can respond with this time period. With this flow, we come up with additional responsibilities for the PizzaMaker and the PizzaDeliverer:

- Interface PizzaMaker

    - Determine how long it will take to make a pizza.

- Interface PizzaDeliverer

    - Determine how long it will take to deliver a pizza, assuming it will be ready at a particular time.

OrderEnterer now has interactions with these two interfaces, which we show on the card in Figure 7.5, on the following page.

We could have the PizzaMaker report the time to delivery by asking the PizzaDeliverer for the delivery time. However, that would tie PizzaMaker to PizzaDeliverer. With that coupling, testing will become more complicated.

We can also run through the misuse test cases to see whether we need to assign additional responsibilities. The Place Order to Nonexistent Address misuse case comes to mind. The PizzaDeliverer needs to notify the OrderEnterer if it cannot deliver the pizza because the address does not exist (in compliance with the Third Law of Interfaces). At this point we don't specify the means of notification. When we start designing and coding, we can determine how PizzaDeliverer should report this condition.

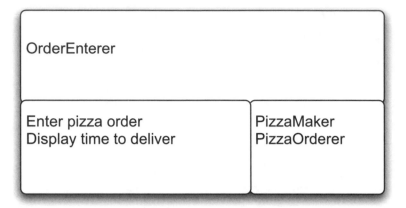

Figure 7.5: IRI CARD WITH INTERACTIONS

7.6 Design

Once we are somewhat satisfied that we have captured the essential concepts and that we can perform the use cases with these abstractions, we can turn these IRI cards into more detailed interfaces. You can write the interface declarations directly in your language of choice, or you can put the interface definitions into some design tool and let it generate the initial code. Many of the responsibilities show up as methods in the corresponding interfaces:

```
enumeration Topping {MUSHROOMS, PEPPERONI, ...};
enumeration Size {SMALL, MEDIUM, LARGE};
interface Pizza
    Size size
    Topping [] toppings
interface Address
    String street
    String city
    String zip
    String phone_number
    DistanceInMiles distance_to_address(Address another)
interface Order
    Pizza
    Address
interface OrderEnterer
    TimePeriod enter_order(Order) signals AddressOutOfDeliveryArea
interface PizzaMaker
    TimePeriod time_to_be_ready(Order)
    place_order(Order)
```

Configuration Is Yet Another Interface

Most programs are not completely static. The end user should be able to change some facets of a system without involving the developer. Although for simplicity we showed Size and Toppings as enumerations in the previous interface definitions, most likely these will need to change. These changes can be handled by a configuration interface. For example:

```
interface Configuration
    Size [] get_pizza_sizes()
    Topping [] get_pizza_toppings()
```

Configuration information may be kept in a file, a database, or an application registry. The Configuration interface hides its actual representation. Alternative configurations can be used for testing. These alternatives may be handled by either replacing the entire representation for a configuration or by adding set methods to the Configuration interface.*

The appendix discusses configuration in more detail.

---

*This configuration works as a Service Locator pattern. You might also use the Dependency Injection pattern for configuration. See http://www.martinfowler.com/articles/injection.html for a discussion on the differences. Fowler appears to favor the Service Locator pattern for application components and Dependency Injection for components that are distributed in general libraries.

```
    Order get_next_order()
interface PizzaDeliverer
    notify_order_ready(Order)
    pay_for_order(Order)
    TimePeriod time_to_deliver(Order, TimePeriod when_ready)
```

The previous definitions are language-independent. You could write the definitions directly in your implementation language. You could create a separate interface definition and then create classes or modules that implement that interface, or you could simply use the interface as the basis for a class. For data interfaces, the latter is the simplest approach. For service interfaces, the former is more flexible, especially for testing, as we shall see.

Getting Something Working

You usually won't be able to take every consideration into account when defining interfaces. You should validate your initial interface design by creating an implementation with the basic responsibilities. This implementation corresponds to the Pragmatic Programmer's *tracer bullets** Following that guideline, you "get something working": an end-to-end implementation of a system. That implementation can help verify that you made a good cut at creating an initial set of interfaces. You can then tweak your design by creating new interfaces, adding methods, altering method parameters, and so forth.

*See the original in *The Pragmatic Programmer: From Journeyman to Master* by Andy Hunt and Dave Thomas (Addison-Wesley Professional, 1999)

Interfaces Outside the Software System

Interfaces and services also apply outside the software realm. We know we need a nonsoftware implementation of a PhysicalPizzaMaker whose job is to actually create the physical pizza. An implementation of this interface may delegate responsibilities to other interfaces, such as the DoughMaker, the DoughThrower, the PizzaCreator, and the PizzaBaker. A real person might implement just the PhysicalPizzaMaker or might implement the other interfaces as well. With all these interfaces that have a smaller set of responsibilities, the implementation for each can be assigned to a different individual. Each individual interface implementation can be independently tested.

An implementation of the PhysicalPizzaMaker might be an automated system. Such a system could make the dough, throw the dough, place toppings on the pizza, put the pizza in the oven, remove the pizza, and put it in a box. When we create tests against the PhysicalPizzaMaker interface, we simply want to ensure that an implementation meets its obligations. The tests should not be dependent on whether humans or machines are making the pizza. You just keep running the tests until the results meet your expectations. This might be fattening.

Testing

Given the explicit methods of the interfaces, we can turn the outline of the tests we have developed directly into code; we'll develop the tests for the interface prior to creating the implementation. If we find that the tests are difficult to create, that is usually a sign that the interface may not be optimal. For example, here's a portion of the test for a Normal Pizza Order:[9]

```
Pizza pizza = new Pizza()
pizza.set_size(SMALL);
Topping [] toppings = {MUSHROOMS};
pizza.set_toppings(toppings);

Address address = new Address();
address.set_street("1 Oak Lane");
address.set_city("Durham");
address.set_zip("27701");
address.set_phone_number("919-555-1212");

Order order = new Order();
order.set_pizza(pizza)
order.set_address(address);

OrderEnterer order_enterer = OrderEntererFactory.get_instance();
TimePeriod time_period = order_enterer.enter_order(order);
AssertNotNull("Time period for order", time_period);
```

When we test this program, it'll be hard to have cooks keep pushing a button saying that a pizza is done. So we'll need to write simulators: implementations that simulate the operations contracted by an interface. For example, here's the interface for PizzaMaker again:

```
interface PizzaMaker
    TimePeriod time_to_be_ready(Order)
    place_order(Order)
    Order get_next_order()
```

A simulator for PizzaMaker would accept an order (place_order()), wait some period of time, and then invoke notify_order_ready() on the PizzaDeliverer interface. A more elaborate simulator might wait an amount of time based on the number of pizzas currently on order. For fast testing purposes, the simulator can be set to respond as quickly as possible.

---

[9]This test code uses the interface methods to set values since we're dealing with interfaces. All these set methods suggest that you might add constructors to the Pizza, Address, and Order classes. The constructors will decrease the code for the test.

Developer testing would be stifled if it took 20 minutes for a response to occur.

7.7 Implementation

As we get into implementing a particular interface, more interfaces may be created. For example, to determine how long till an order is complete, the PizzaMaker will need to keep some queue of Orders in process. The PizzaMaker uses the number of Orders in the queue to determine the amount of time before an order can be started. So in a lower level, we may have an OrderQueue interface. We will create tests for that interface that check that it performs according to its contract.

7.8 Things to Remember

In interface-oriented design, the emphasis is on designing a solution with interfaces. When using IOD, here are some tips:

- Use IRI cards to assign responsibilities to interfaces.

- Keep service interface definitions in code separate from the code for classes that implement it.

- Write tests first to determine the usability of an interface.

- Write tests against the contract for the interface.

Part III

Interfaces in the Real World

Chapter 8

Link Checker

This chapter and the next two present three interface-oriented designs. Each design emphasizes different aspects of interfaces:

- The Link Checker demonstrates using an interface to hide multiple implementations that parse a web page.

- The Web Conglomerator shows how to delegate work among multiple implementations.

- The Service Registry presents a document-style interface and demonstrates some issues with documents.

Having broken links on your web site can annoy your visitors. I'm sure I have had several broken links on mine; the Net is an ever-changing place. A link checker that ensures all links are working is a valuable tool to keep your visitors happy. In this chapter, we'll create a link checker, and along the way, we'll see how designing with interfaces allows for a variety of easily testable implementations.

8.1 Vision

The vision for this system is short and sweet. The link checker examines links in the pages of a web site to see whether they refer to active pages. It identifies links that are broken.

8.2 Conceptualization

It's always a good idea to try to get definitions straight at the beginning. We consider the two types of links and one variation. The user is going to specify a domain, as "www.pughkilleen.com," or a URL that includes

---

Figure 8.1: USE CASE FOR LINK CHECKER

---

a domain, such as "www.pughkilleen.com/classes.html." An *internal link* is a link to a page with the same domain as the specified one. An *external link* has a different domain. A variation on a link is one with an anchor. An *anchor* is a specific location within a web page, denoted by a label following a #, such as "www.pughkilleen.com/classes.html#Java." We should examine the referenced web page to see whether the anchor exists in that page. To keep the first iteration short, we will save that aspect to the next iteration.

The single use case is as follows:

Use Case: Check Links on URL

1. User enters a URL.

2. The system reports all broken internal and external links on all pages in the domain that can be reached from the URL.

Even with one use case, a use case diagram such as Figure 8.1 is often a nice way to depict what interactions a system has with outside actors.

Let's describe in more detail the work that the system will perform in response to the entered URL.

Use Case: Check Links on URL

1. User enters a URL.

2. The system determines the domain from the URL.

3. The system retrieves the page for the URL from the appropriate web server.

4. The system examines the retrieved page for internal and external links:

    a) For internal links, the system recursively retrieves the page for each link and examines that page for links.

    b) If a link is broken, the system reports it.

    c) For external links, the system just retrieves the page to see whether it is accessible.

5. The system stops when all internal links and external links have been examined.

Since this GUI is really basic, a prototype report can help developers and users visualize the results of the use case. We present an outline of a report here:

Prototype Report

```
Domain:  a_domain.com
   Page: a_domain.com/index.html
       Internal Broken Link(s)
           Page: whatsup.html
           Page: notmuch.html
       External Broken Link(s):
           Page: www.somewhere-else.com/nothingdoing.html
           Page: www.somewhere-else.com/not_here.html
```

8.3 Analysis

Based on the conceptualization, we come up with a number of responsibilities and assign them to interfaces using IRI cards. We follow the guideline from Chapter 7 to decouple interfaces that may be implemented differently. We know we need to retrieve pages, so we create a WebPageRetriever interface that returns WebPages. We need to parse a WebPage into links, so we add a WebPageParser. We include a LinkRepository to keep track of the links. The IRI cards we come up with appear in Figure 8.2, on the following page. Each of the interfaces has clearly defined responsibilities.

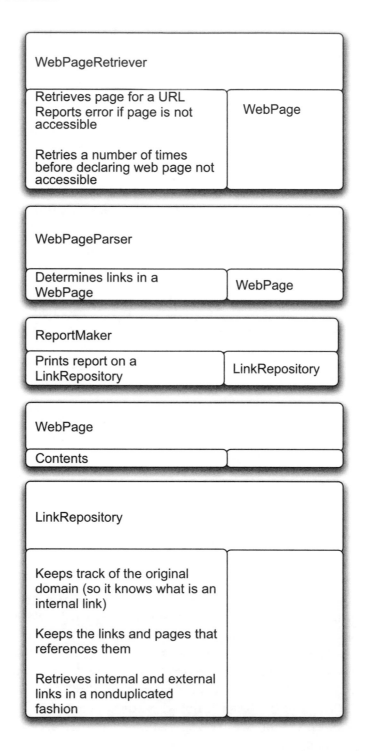

Figure 8.2: IRI CARDS

8.4 Design

We take the interfaces on the IRI cards and develop them into more specific methods.

The Web Page

WebPage is just a data interface:

```
interface WebPage
    set_url(URL)
    set_contents(String)
    String get_contents()
```

Parsing the Web Page

WebPageParser has a single method:

```
interface WebPageParser
    URL [] parse_for_URLs(WebPage)
```

At this point, we're not sure how we are going to parse a web page into links. We could use a regular expression parser. We could use SAX or DOM (Chapter 3), if the web pages are well-formed. Or we could use javax.swing.text.html.parser.Parser, which parses most web pages. Having this interface allows us to easily test whatever implementation we decide to use. There is not much of a contract to enforce (Chapter 2). The contractual tests consist of passing web pages with a variety of content and checking that all the links are returned.

Using this interface decouples the implementation from the tests. If we create a second implementation, we can use the same functional tests. If we want to compare the two implementations for speed or ability to handle poorly formed input, we write the tests against this interface.

Having the interface makes selecting an implementation less critical. We pick one. If it's too slow, we pick another. The code that requires the parsing does not need to be changed.

The WebPageParser returns an array of URLs.[1] This URL interface contains mostly data:

```
data interface URL
    protocol (e.g., http://)
```

---

[1]If you're familiar with Java, you may recall that the Java library has a URL class.

Multiple Implementations

Creating multiple implementations of the same interface is often employed in high-reliability software. For example, three teams each code an airplane guidance module. Each team uses a different algorithm; another module compares the results of the three. If they all agree, the comparison module uses that value. If fewer than three agree, the module signals a problem to the pilot. If only two agree on a value, the comparison module uses that value. If none of them agree, the comparison module has to make a decision. It might default to using the one module that agreed most in the past with the other two modules.

```
domain (e.g., www.pughkilleen.com)
port (optional, e.g., :8080)
file (e.g., /index.html)
anchor (optional, comes after '#')
additional (optional, comes after '?')
to_string() // returns string of URL
from_string(String) // parses string into URL
```

Retrieving the Web Page

The WebPageRetriever retrieves the WebPage corresponding to a particular URL. We don't want to report that a link is bad if there is just a temporary failure in the Internet. So, WebPageRetriever could signal an error if it cannot locate the URL in a reasonable number of tries, rather than in a single try. It has a single method:

```
interface WebPageRetriever
    WebPage retrieve_page(URL) signals UnableToContactDomain,
        UnableToFindPage
```

Storing the Links

The LinkRepository stores the URLs that have been found in retrieved pages. It needs to know the base domain so that it can distinguish internal links from external links. LinkRepository also records which URLs are broken and which are OK. LinkRepository is probably going to create a type of object (say a Link), which contains the URL and this information. But we really don't care how it performs its responsibilities. We just want it to do its job, which is defined like so:

Combining Interfaces

We could add retrieve() and parse() methods to Webpage to make it have more behavior. Those methods would delegate to WebPageParser and WebPageRetriever the jobs of retrieving and parsing the page. The interface would look like this:

```
interface WebPage
    set_url(URL)
    set_contents(String)
    String get_contents()
    retrieve()
    URL [] parse_for_URLs()
```

The methods are cohesive in the sense that they all deal with a WebPage. Initially, we'll keep the interfaces separate to simplify testing. Later we can add the methods to WebPage. At that point, we'll need to decide how flexible we want to be. If the implementations for WebPageParser and WebPageRetriever should be changeable, we can set up a configuration interface, which is called when a WebPage is constructed:

```
interface WebPageConfiguration
    WebPageParser get_web_page_parser()
    WebPageRetriever get_web_page_retriever()
```

Alternatively, we can use the Dependency Injection (Inversion of Control) pattern* to set up the implementations. With this pattern, we supply the WebPage with the desired implementations:

```
interface WebPage
    set_parser(WebPageParser)
    set_retriever(WebPageRetriever)
    set_url(URL)
    set_contents(String)
    String get_contents()
    retrieve()
    URL [] parse_for_URLs()
```

USING CONFIGURATION
>   Advantage—hides implementation requirements

>   Disadvantage—services have dependency on a configuration interface

USING INVERSION OF CONTROL
>   Advantage—common feature (used in frameworks)

>   Disadvantage—can be harder to understand

---

*See http://martinfowler.com/articles/injection.html for more details.

```
interface LinkRepository
    set_base_domain(Domain base_domain)
    add_URL(URL link, URL reference )
        // adds reference (web page that it comes from)
    URL get_next_internal_link()
        // null if no more links
    URL get_next_external_link()
        // null if no more links
    set_URL_as_broken(URL)
    set_URL_as_okay(URL)
```

LinkRepository has a more complicated contract than WebPageRetriever. For example, if you already know the status of the link, you don't want a URL to be returned by get_next_internal_link(). So, you need to check that LinkRepository properly returns the URLs that have not already been retrieved, regardless of how many times they may be referenced.

You should review your interfaces before you implement them. Otherwise, you may implement methods that turn out to be useless.[2] We could add to LinkRepository the job of cycling through the links, retrieving the pages, and parsing the pages. Its current responsibilities center on differentiating between internal and external links and retrieving them in a nonduplicated manner.

We could add a push-style interface to LinkRepository (see Chapter 3) to perform the operation of cycling through the links. The push style in this instance is somewhat more complicated. The method that is called may add additional entries into the LinkRepository that invoked it. So, we'll start with pull style. Shortly, we'll create another interface that actually does the pulling.

We probably want an add_URLs(URL [ ] links, URL reference)[3] as a convenience method. After all, we are retrieving sets of URLs from pages, not just a single URL. So, making a more complete interface simplifies its use.

The two get_next() methods return links that haven't yet been retrieved. If a link is internal, we are going to retrieve the page, parse it, and add the new links to the LinkRepository. If a link is external, we are just going to retrieve the page to see whether it exists, but not parse it. Now that sounds like we might want to have an additional interface (say Link) with two implementations: ExternalLink and InternalLink. They would contain a

---

[2]Thanks to Rob Walsh for this thought. He adds "or completely wrong."

[3]Do the parameters in the method seem reversed? Should the links go after the reference? Making the order consistent with every code reviewer's idea of correct order is impossible, as you can probably imagine.

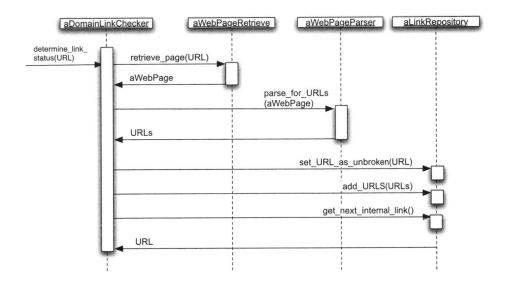

Figure 8.3: Sequence diagram (for internal links that are not broken)

process method that implements the different steps we just noted. We leave that alteration as an exercise to the reader.

Controlling the Cycling

We create a separate control interface (see Chapter 3), called Domain-LinkChecker, for the logic that goes through each link, retrieves it, and checks it. It's going to need a LinkRepository into which to put all the links. Alternatively, DomainLinkChecker could return to us a LinkRepository. The former is simpler, the latter more complex (see Chapter 4). One reason for passing the LinkRepository is that we could record the link status for multiple URLs in the same repository.

```
interface DomainLinkChecker

    set_link_repository(LinkRepository)
    determine_link_status(URL beginning_url)
        // Recursively cycles through links
```

Figure 8.3 illustrates a sequence diagram for determine_link_status(). It depicts how the interfaces we have introduced so far interact.

Creating the Report

Once determine_link_status( ) is finished, we need to turn the information in LinkRepository into a report. Decoupling the gathering of the information from the presentation of the information not only gives flexibility but also makes testing easier. We can populate a LinkRepository with some known data and produce a report from it. We have a ReportMaker interface that takes the information in LinkRepository and forms it into the desired output. If this were a web-based link checker, this Report-Maker could produce an HTML page, or we could employ JavaServer Pages (JSPs) or Active Server Pages (ASPs) to generate the pages.

```
interface ReportMaker
    set_link_repository(LinkRepository)
    String get_output()  // returns text stream
```

Currently, LinkRepository has no methods for retrieving information. We need to add some, but in what form or order should the information be retrieved? We have a prototype report that is in web page order with internal and external links underneath the referencing page. However, that report is only a prototype, and we do not want to couple the sequence of retrieval for LinkRepository to that particular report.

Introducing another data interface provides this decoupling. The report needs the following information for each link:

```
interface LinkReference
    URL referring_page
    URL referred_to_page
    Type    {INTERNAL or EXTERNAL}
    Broken {YES, NO, UNDETERMINED}
```

LinkReferences are kept in a LinkReferenceCollection. We give LinkReferenceCollection the responsibility of returning the LinkReferences in the desired order. So, we put all LinkReference sorting as part of a LinkReferenceCollection. If another user wants to access the links in the same order, the sort can be reused. If not, the user can add another sort method to the collection.

```
interface LinkReferenceCollection
    sort_by_referring_page()
    sort_by_referred_to_page()
    LinkReference get_next_link_reference()
    add_link_reference(LinkReference)
```

We can use this data interface to simplify testing. You can create a LinkReferenceCollection, fill it in with some data, and then use Report-Maker to print a report. You can work with your users to create a report

---

Simple or Complex?

You may have noted that LinkReferenceCollection contains two methods for sorting the collection:

```
interface LinkReferenceCollection
    sort_by_referring_page()
    sort_by_referred_to_page()
```

This is an example of a simple interface (see Chapter 4). The sort methods are supplied to the user; they do not have to do any additional coding. However, they are limited to those sorts. As an alternative, we could provide a more complex interface:

```
interface LinkReferenceComparator
    boolean greater_than(LinkReference one, LinkReference two)


interface LinkReferenceCollection
    sort_your_way(LinkReferenceComparator)
```

With sort_your_way(), the user provides a greater_than() that compares to LinkReferences and returns an indication of which should come later in the sort order. This is a little more complex, but a lot more flexible.

---

that matches their needs. You'll also create tests on LinkRepository to check that it can produce the proper data in a LinkReferenceCollection.

With the LinkReferenceCollection, LinkRepository needs a method:

```
LinkReferenceCollection get_link_reference_collection()
```

Now the ReportMaker really needs only a LinkReferenceCollection, rather than the entire LinkRepository, so let's change its interface to the following:

```
interface ReportMaker
    set_link_reference_collection(LinkReferenceCollection)
    String get_output()  // returns text stream
```

8.5 Tests

Before starting implementation, we create an outline of the tests to be run against these interfaces. We derive these tests from the workflow introduced in the "Analysis" section. The tests may yield insights into the degree of coupling between the interfaces.

- WebPage

    - This class does not have much to test. It just has get and set methods.

- WebPageParser

    - Create a WebPageParser, and parse several different WebPages.

    - Check to see that the links agree with manually identified links on these pages.

- URL

    - Create some URLs, and see whether the parts match manually identified parts.

- LinkReferenceCollection

    - Add some LinkReferences, sort them, and see whether results are correct.

- LinkRepository

    - Add URLs to the repository.

        * Check that the next_link() methods return the appropriate values.

    - Add URLs to the repository.

        * Set some as broken.

        * Check to see list of broken links in LinkReferenceCollection matches expectations.

- WebPageRetriever

    - Retrieve some web pages, both internal and external, existing and nonexisting, and see whether results are as expected.

- ReportMaker

    - Print report on a LinkReferenceCollection (e.g., as created in the LinkReferenceCollection test), and see whether the user agrees with its format.

Since there are few dependencies in these tests, the interfaces are loosely coupled. LinkRepository does not perform the URL retrieval, so it is not coupled to WebPageRetriever or WebPageParser. If LinkRepository were coupled to these interfaces, we would either have to create stub implementations for these two interfaces or wait until the real implementation was complete before testing LinkRepository. This easier testing procedure supports our design choice.

The tests suggest an order for creation. URL and WebPage should be completed first; WebPageRetriever, WebPageParser, and LinkRepository can be done in parallel. LinkReferenceCollection should be created prior to ReportMaker. Then the developer for ReportMaker can work with the end user to determine the actual layout.

8.6 Implementation

We discussed in Chapter 2 that an interface definition is not complete until there is at least one implementation of the interface. But my publisher does not want me to fill up this book with code; he says the purpose of web sites is to provide code, so the full implementation of the Link Checker appears at the URL listed in the preface.

Using interface-oriented design, just as with other techniques, does not guarantee that you'll never have to restructure your interfaces or refactor your code. As you develop a system, you usually discover additional information that suggests a restructuring of the design.

For example, the tests for the system revealed that links in a web page are not just links to other web pages.[4] The links may be links to email addresses ("mailto"), file transfer links ("ftp"), or other types of links. Now comes the question: what to do with these links? How do you check a "mailto"? Do you send the address a message? Do you see whether the address is invalid? Do you wait for a response from the recipient? File transfer links are a little easier. You could attempt to retrieve the file. Even if the file were an internal link, you probably would not want to parse the file for links.

Separating policy decisions from implementation can permit greater reuse of interfaces and implementations. LinkRepository can store the links, regardless of the type. Indeed, that is how these other links were revealed. DomainLinkChecker can decide what to do with these other links when it retrieves one from LinkRepository. We can add to the URL interface a method that tells us the type of link, we can retrieve that

---

[4]You probably knew this already, like I did, but it was absent from my mind until running the tests.

information from the URL and perform the test ourselves, or we can create yet another interface.[5]

The Code

The system is coded in Java, since that's a common language and readily understood by most object-oriented programmers. The method names have been changed to camel case to conform to typical Java coding standards. Since exceptions are a widespread way of signaling in Java, the error signals are thrown exceptions. Separate exceptions were thrown for each type of error that the caller may want to deal with differently.

To keep the code simple, interface implementations are created in the code itself, rather than by calling a factory method. The following is the code for the main routine. It reads the initial URL from the command line. ReportMakerSimple produces tab-delimited output, suitable for import in a spreadsheet or other data manipulation program.[6]

```java
public class LinkChecker
    {
    public static void main(String[] args)
        {
        if (args.length >= 1)
            {
            try
                {
                MyURL initialURL = new MyURL(args[0]);

                DomainLinkChecker checker =
                    new DomainLinkCheckerImplementation();
                LinkRepository repository =
                    new LinkRepositoryImplementation();

                checker.setLinkRepository(repository);
                checker.determineLinkStatus(initialURL);
                LinkReferenceCollection linkRefColl =
                    repository.getLinkReferenceCollection();

                ReportMaker reportMaker = new ReportMakerSimple();
                reportMaker.SetLinkReferenceCollection(linkRefColl);
                String output = reportMaker.getOutput();

                // Could print it to a file
```

---

[5]We leave that decision for the reader to pursue.

[6]I renamed the URL class to MyURL to keep it distinct from the Java URL class. The underlying code delegates most of its work to the Java library class.

```
            System.out.println(output);
            }
        catch (BadPageDeviation e)
            {
            System.out.println("Bad URL " + args[0]);
            }
        }
    else
        {
        System.out.println("You must specify the initial URL");
        }
    }
}
```

Here's the implementation of DomainLinkChecker. Note that it has two loops, one for internal links and one for external links. The system does not parse external web pages for additional links.[7]

```
public class DomainLinkCheckerImplementation implements DomainLinkChecker
  {
  private LinkRepository linkRepository;

  public void setLinkRepository(LinkRepository aRepository)
    {
    linkRepository = aRepository;
    }

  public void determineLinkStatus(MyURL beginningURL)
    {
    linkRepository.setBaseDomain(beginningURL);
    WebPageRetriever webPageRetriever = new WebPageRetrieverUsingURL();
    WebPageParser webPageParser = new WebPageParserByRegEx();

    MyURL currentURL = beginningURL;
    linkRepository.addURL(currentURL, currentURL);
    linkRepository.setURLAsRetrieved(currentURL);

    // Internal Links
    while (currentURL != null)
      {
      try
        {
        if (!currentURL.isHTTP())
            continue;
        WebPage webPage = webPageRetriever.retrievePage(currentURL);
        linkRepository.setURLAsNotBroken(currentURL);
```

_____

[7]What if you wanted to check all external web pages to ensure that any links that pointed to your site were not broken? The design and implementation of that system is left as an exercise to the reader.

```
            MyURL[] urls = webPageParser.parseForURLs(webPage);
            linkRepository.addURLs(urls, currentURL);
            }
        catch (UnableToContactDomainDeviation e)
            {
            System.out.println("Unable to find page " + currentURL);
            // Cannot contact our own domain - might as well leave
            return;
            }
        catch (UnableToFindPageDeviation e)
            {
            linkRepository.setURLAsBroken(currentURL);
            }
        finally
            {
            currentURL = linkRepository.getNextUnretrievedInternalLink();
            }
        }

    // External Links
    currentURL = linkRepository.getNextUnretrievedExternalLink();
    while (currentURL != null)
        {
        try
            {
            WebPage webPage = webPageRetriever.retrievePage(currentURL);
            linkRepository.setURLAsNotBroken(currentURL);
            }
        catch (UnableToContactDomainDeviation e)
            {
            linkRepository.setURLAsBroken(currentURL);
            }
        catch (UnableToFindPageDeviation e)
            {
            linkRepository.setURLAsBroken(currentURL);
            }
        finally
            {
            currentURL = linkRepository.getNextUnretrievedExternalLink();
            }
        }
    return;
    }
}
```

Can this code be refactored? Your code style sense may suggest refactoring. With the clearly defined interfaces handling most of the work, you can easily make changes to this code.

GUI Ideas

You can readily adapt this code to use in a GUI. The code in the main()
method can become the code for the method of an interface such as
LinkChecker:

```
interface LinkChecker
       String check_links(MyURL url)
```

You can set up a dialog box that contains a text field for a URL and
a submit button. Clicking the button invokes the check_links() method.
The string returned by the method can be displayed in an edit box or a
separate window.

A GUI often has some sort of feedback mechanism to indicate to the
user that progress is being made. We can use a callback interface
(push-style interface from Chapter 3) to perform the feedback. We need
to make minor changes in the interfaces to pass a callback method.
Every time a new link is accessed, the current_link() method is called.
The method could display the name in a read-only text box.

```
interface LinkCheckerCallback
       current_link(MyURL link)

interface DomainLinkChecker
    determineLinkStatus(MyURL url, LinkCheckerCallback)

interface LinkChecker
       String check_links(MyURL url, LinkCheckerCallback )
```

8.7 Retrospective

Separating responsibilities into several interfaces allows these interfaces to be employed in programs other than the one presented in this
chapter. For example, since web page retrieval has been separated from
the parsing, you can employ these classes in a web page (HTML) edit-
ing program. You can use WebPageParser to obtain links referenced in
a page for display in a window.

8.8 Things to Remember

The Link Checker demonstrated the following:

• Use IRI cards as an interface design tool.

- Create decoupled implementations with interfaces.

- Separate responsibilities to make simpler interfaces.

- Write tests against interfaces, rather than against particular implementations, to allow for test reuse.

Chapter 9

Web Conglomerator

We're going to create an interface-oriented design for a web-based application. A common development question is, when should you make a design more general? In this application, we'll show one case of transforming a specific interface into a more general one and one case where that transformation is deferred.

9.1 Vision

The Web Conglomerator is your own custom browsing portal. Many web sites offer the ability to customize a web page with the information in which you have an interest. The Web Conglomerator performs this service on your machine. It presents a custom web page to you with content derived from many sites. The example in this chapter specifically shows travel-related information, but the information could be about anything from the stock market to butterflies.

9.2 Conceptualization

We have only two use cases for the Web Conglomerator (See Figure 9.1, on the following page): to configure the system and to request a current display.[1]

Here are descriptions for both of the use cases:

---

[1]As a side note, the system should be arranged so the user must request an update of the page. Creating a system that automatically updates places a burden on the information providers.

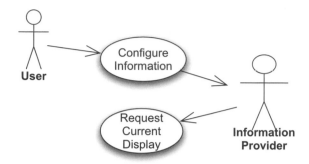

Figure 9.1: USE CASES

 Use Case: Configure Information

1. User determines the blocks of information to be presented.

2. System stores the configuration information.

 Use Case: Request Current Display

1. User requests that the Web Conglomerator display the current page.

2. System responds with a page containing the current information.

GUI prototypes help both the developer and the user understand the intended operation of a system. So, we prototype what our travel-related conglomerator may look like (other forms of information could easily be conglomerated as well).

From the user's viewpoint, he initially loads a page into his browser, say `localhost:8080//travel.html`. The browser displays that page, as shown in Figure 9.2, on the next page. When the user submits a search for a city or ZIP code, the browser contacts the web conglomerator, which returns a page with the information corresponding to the display. The web conglomerator creates the web page from content provided by either web services or other web pages, or both.

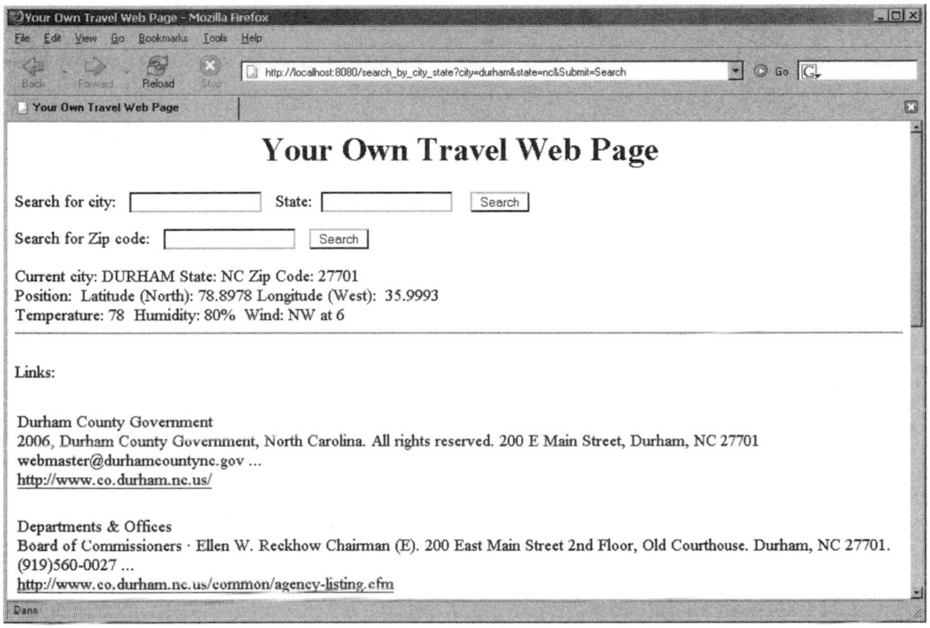

Figure 9.2: WEB BROWSER RESULTS

9.3 Analysis

Let's create some IRI cards for potential interfaces. We stated that we are going to display the information in a web browser. However, the display of information should not be coupled to how we obtain the information. Otherwise, changing a provider for a piece of information can have ramifications throughout the system. So, we create data gatherer interfaces, as well as data formatter interfaces. Instead of showing the actual cards, we save a little paper and just list the proposed interfaces:

- IndividualDataGatherer

  - Retrieves one type of information (e.g., weather) from an information provider

- IndividualDataFormatter

  - Formats information of a single information type

- WebConglomerator

  - Formats information from IndividualDataFormatters

These interfaces may seem a bit too abstract to help us really understand the system. So, using the prototype page in the previous section, let's examine the data we need to gather in a concrete instance. The only caveat is that we do not want to limit ourselves to a particular type of information. Generalization of these interfaces can be deferred to a later time. We just want to keep in mind that if interfaces may be generalized, we do not make any decisions that would obviously make that generalization harder.

A Concrete Gatherer

We do a little checking of potential sources for weather information for a DataGatherer. It turns out that if you do not have a recognizable city, some sources return either an error message or a multiple-choice selection. However, all the sources can use a ZIP code to uniquely identify a location. So, the first step in obtaining weather information is to find the ZIP code for a location.

So we start with a LocationFinder to obtain the ZIP code or the city/state if a ZIP code is entered. This initial interface looks like this:

```
data interface Location
    City
    State
    Zip
interface LocationFinder
    Location find_by_city_state(City, State) signals LocationNotFound
    Location find_by_zip(Zip) signals LocationNotFound
```

The Location data can be used by any of the other DataGatherers. When either a city/state or a ZIP code is entered on the initial screen, this interface can provide the ZIP code.

Using the Location, we obtain weather information. We break the data into two interfaces to make a cohesive Wind interface, rather than having WindSpeed and WindDirection be part of WeatherInformation:

```
data interface Wind
    Direction
    Speed
data interface WeatherInformation
    Temperature
    Humidity
    Wind
interface WeatherInformationDataGatherer
    WeatherInformation find_by_location(Location)
```

We create more interfaces to retrieve other information on a particular location:

```
data interface PositionInformation
    Longitude
    Latitude
interface PositionInformationDataGatherer
    PositionInformation find_by_location(Location)

data interface TimeInformation
    Time
    TimeZone
interface TimeInformationDataGatherer
    TimeInformation find_by_location(Location)
```

The final interface is the one that searches for web page links to the selected Location. If we want to use multiple link sources, the underlying implementation simply combines the links from each service using some internal mechanism.

```
data interface WebPageLink
    Title
    Description
    URL

interface WebPageLinkDataGatherer
    WebPageLink [] get_links_for_location(Location)
```

Corresponding to each of these DataGatherers is a DataFormatter. For example, we have this:

```
interface WeatherInformationDataFormatter
    String format_for_html_display(WeatherInformation)
```

We recognize that there may be a common interface for DataGatherers and DataFormatters. We'll come back to that issue shortly. Let's take a look at how these interfaces interact to offer the conglomeration feature. Here is the interface for the page to be displayed and for the WebConglomerator itself:

```
interface CustomWebPage
    add_html(String html_to_add)
    String get_contents()

interface WebConglomerator
    CustomWebPage find_by_city_state(City, State)
    CustomWebPage find_by_zip_code(ZipCode)
```

To form a CustomWebPage, each DataGatherer is given the Location. Then the DataFormatter is used to form HTML strings. Those strings

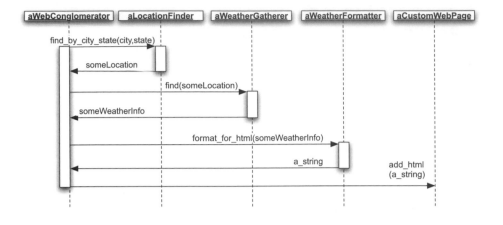

Figure 9.3: SEQUENCE DIAGRAM FOR THE WEB CONGLOMERATOR

are then added to the CustomWebPage. A sequence diagram for the interactions between these interfaces appears in Figure 9.3.

9.4 Testing

Before continuing to design, we outline some tests to be run against these interfaces. Creating tests can point out coupling issues.[2]

- DataGatherer

  - Check that the information returned by find_by_location()matches information from other sources. Because of the dynamic nature of the data, we may need to create two implementations of DataGatherer and compare the data returned.[3]

- DataFormatter

  - Put the display strings into a simple HTML file, and see whether the output is displayed in a readable form.

- WebPageLinkDataGatherer

  - Check that the number of links and the data in each one correspond to the information from the search results.

---

[2]A tester noted that not all these tests might be automated.
[3]See the "Multiple Implementations" sidebar in Chapter 8.

- WebConglomerator

    - See whether the page displays the same information as the individual DataFormatters.

We will want implementations of DataGatherer that return constant information for testing other classes. We need to set up some type of configuration mechanism to switch between these constant test implementations and the real implementations.[4]

One situation we come up with is that a DataGatherer may be unable to obtain the data because of network or provider problems. We need to have the find_by_location() method signal that it is unable to obtain the data in accordance with the Third Law of Interfaces. If there were multiple providers for the same information, the DataGatherer can attempt to retrieve the data from all of them before signaling an error.

A couple of other situations that we'll need to handle are the user entering a city and/or a state that LocationFinder cannot find and the user entering a ZIP code for which a particular DataGatherer has no information. We'll be sure to test these cases. In any event, we want to be sure that the output contains an indication that the information is unavailable (again in accordance with the Third Law of Interfaces).

9.5 Design

We think we are ready to begin filling in some of the details. In the analysis of the previous section, we discussed that the information gathering ought to be generalized. Let's look at how we might accomplish this. Two interfaces, each with a single method, appear for each of the types of information. The WebConglomerator should not care what type of information is being gathered or displayed. So, we make up an InformationTransformer interface:

```
interface InformationTransformer
    gather_data_for_location(Location)
        signals DataUnavailable
    String format_for_html_display()
```

---

[4]The configuration can be done by each DataGatherer using a common configuration interface, or we can use Inversion of Control, as discussed in the sidebar in Chapter 8. (See also http://www.martinfowler.com/articles/injection.html for details.) That's an implementation decision that could go either way, depending on complexity.

Individual information transformers can implement this interface. We keep the gathering of the data separate from the formatting, because those are two distinct operations. For example:

```
interface WeatherInformationTransformer implements
    InformationTransformer
    gather_data_for_location(Location) signals DataUnavailable
    String format_for_html_display()
```

The implementation of this interface uses WeatherInformation, WeatherInformationDataGatherer, and WeatherInformationDataFormatter. Although those interfaces are not visible in WeatherInformationTransformer, keeping them as separate interfaces can make testing them easier. You can test multiple WeatherInformationDataGatherers against each other by comparing the WeatherInformation returned by each of them.[5]

The WebConglomerator now can contain a collection of InformationTransformers. It gathers data from each one, formats it, and then adds it to the CustomWebPage. Configuring WebConglomerator (the other use case) simply involves adding or deleting InformationTransformers from this collection.

You may note that the InformationTransformer interface shown previously is stateful (see Chapter 3). The gather_data_for_location() method gets information that is later output by format_for_html_display(). We could turn it into a stateless interface:

```
interface InformationTransformer
    String get_html_formatted_data_for_location(Location)
        signals DataUnavailable
```

With the first version, we separated the retrieval of the data from the display of the data. That makes the interface easier to test. However, using this interface makes it simpler from the user's standpoint: there's only one method to call. As discussed in Chapter 3, we could implement this stateless interface by calling the stateful one, if a simpler interface was desired.

Web Retrieval: A Textual Interface

We could use WebConglomerator in a stand-alone program. We could have a dialog box to input the city and state, pass those to the WebConglomerator, and then display the results in an HTML-aware text box.

---

[5]If the information is not the same, then you'll have to figure out who provides the most reliable and up-to-date information.

If we employ a browser to display the page, we are going to use a textual protocol (see Chapter 1) to communicate between the browser and a web server. The protocol is HTTP, which consists of a request and a response.[6]

We need to run an implementation of a WebPageServer on the user's local machine. Any implementation of a WebPageServer that follows the contract for HTTP can deliver the custom web page. The browser will point to this server (e.g., `http://localhost:8080/`). The WebPage-Server calls WebConglomerator to create the CustomWebPage and delivers it to the user.

The essential aspects of HTTP that need to be implemented to deliver a CustomWebPage are as follows:[7]

HTTP REQUEST
```
    GET url HTTP/1.0
```

HTTP RESPONSE
```
    HTTP/1.0 200 Success

    Contents of url
```

The url after the GET reflects either an initial page display or the result of a submit button. The three possible value for url for this system are as follows:

```
/
search_by_zipcode?zipcode=27701
search_by_city_state?city=Durham&state=NC
```

The URL / represents the initial page. Based on the value following GET, the WebPageServer returns a page that contains just a search form, or it returns what WebConglomerator has created.

9.6 Implementation

This design has two interesting implementation issues: the WebPage-Server and the DataGatherers. Let's look at each.

We have multiple options for implementing WebPageServer. We want the system to work even if the user does not have access to a web

---

[6]See `http://www.w3.org/Protocols/rfc2616/rfc2616.html` for more details.

[7]If you are implementing a full web server, then you need to handle more commands and options. However, an implementation that just handled these messages can be used as a simple web server.

server that they can customize. We could install an existing web server implementation that supports server-side applications, such as Tomcat, on the user's computer. In that case, we would create a servlet that responds to the request by calling WebConglomerator.

Alternatively, we could write our own WebPageServer that processes just the three variations of a request. If we were distributing WebConglomerator to a wide audience, creating a small server that handles just these requests avoids having a user install a full-blown web server. The code available from the web site[8] contains a small web server.

The other interface are the DataGatherers, such as:

```
interface WeatherInformationDataGatherer
    WeatherInformation find_by_location(Location)
        signals DataUnavailable
```

This interface decouples the information from the means used to get it. An implementation of this interface may access a web service that provides the information. Alternatively, it might retrieve a web page that contains the data and parse that page to find the desired information. It might communicate to a data provider via a custom protocol. The coupling between the user of the interface and the implementation is just WeatherInformation.

The following is the code for WebConglomerator. You may notice that it does not catch a DataUnavailable exception. Instead, each individual InformationTransformer indicates that data is unavailable by placing "N/A" into the returned HTML. The Third Law of Interfaces does not require a particular type of signal. It just requires that an implementation indicate that there was a problem.

```
public class WebConglomeratorImplementation implements WebConglomerator
    {
    LocationInformationTransformer[] transformers = {
        new PositionInformationTransformer(),
        new WeatherInformationTransformer(),
        new WebPageLinkInformationTransformer()
        }

    public CustomWebPage findByCityState(String city, String state)
        {
        LocationFinder finder = new LocationFinderImplementation();
        CustomWebPage webPage;
```

---

[8]See the preface for the URL.

```
    try
        {
        Location location = finder.find_by_city_state(city, state);
        webPage = createCustomWebPage(location);
        }
    catch (LocationNotFound e)
        {
        webPage = getErrorPage("Location Not Found");
        }
    catch (CommunicationException e)
        {
        webPage = getErrorPage(e.getMessage());
        }
    return webPage;
    }

private CustomWebPage createCustomWebPage(Location location)
    {
    for (int i = 0; i < transformers.length; i++)
        {
        transformers[i].gatherDataForLocation(location);
        }
    CustomWebPage webPage = new CustomWebPage();
    StringBuffer contents = new StringBuffer();
    contents = originalPageHeader();
    contents.append(new LocationInformationFormatter().
        formatForHTMLDisplay(location));
    for (int i = 0; i < transformers.length; i++)
        {
        contents.append("<td><tr>");
        contents.append(transformers[i].formatForHTMLDisplay());
        contents.append("</td></tr>");
        }
    contents.append(originalPageFooter());
    webPage.setContents(contents.toString());
    return webPage;
    }
private CustomWebPage getErrorPage(String message)
    {
    CustomWebPage webPage = new CustomWebPage();
    StringBuffer contents = new StringBuffer();
    contents = originalPageHeader();
    contents.append(message);
    contents.append(originalPageFooter());
    webPage.setContents(contents.toString());
    return webPage;
    }
public CustomWebPage getOriginalPage()
    {
    CustomWebPage webPage = new CustomWebPage();
    StringBuffer contents = new StringBuffer();
```

```
        contents = originalPageHeader();
        contents.append(originalPageFooter());
        webPage.setContents(contents.toString());
        return webPage;
        }
}
```

For the most part, the methods follow the interfaces introduced in this chapter. The originalPageHeader() and originalPageFooter() methods return HTML for the header and the footer of the page. The header contains the search form. LocationInformationFormatter formats in HTML, with the Location passed to it.

This code does not implement the first use case—Configure Information. Configuration consists of adding, removing, or rearranging the order of InformationTransformers. In the code that is shown, these values are fixed. You need to create a collection of InformationTransformers and a web interface or a stand-alone program that manipulates that collection. Collections are fairly standard components in language libraries. You can just use the interface to that collection.[9]

9.7   Retrospective

We decided to "get something working" before examining how to make WebConglomerator more general. The current design appears to work well for gathering location-based information. If we want to gather information relating to items, such as stocks or sports teams, we can employ the same general framework. The InformationTransformer and WebConglomerator interfaces have to change. Those interfaces specifically required location-related parameters:

```
interface InformationTransformer
    gather_data_for_location(Location)
        signals DataUnavailable
    String format_for_html_display()

interface WebConglomerator
    CustomWebPage find_by_city_state(City, State)
    CustomWebPage find_by_zip_code(ZipCode)
```

We first could rename these interfaces to LocationInformationTransformer and LocationWebConglomerator. Then we make up equivalent interfaces

---

[9]The appendix shows one approach for creating a custom interface to a collection of InformationTransformers.

for the new items, such as StockInformationTransformer. We may need a StockFinder that parallels LocationFinder. The StockFinder would find a stock ticker given a company name. The interfaces could look like this:

```
data interface Stock
    Ticker
    CompanyName

interface StockFinder
    Stock find_by_ticker(Ticker) signals StockNotFound
    Stock find_by_name(CompanyName) signals StockNotFound

interface StockInformationTransformer
    gather_data_for_stock(Stock)
        signals DataUnavailable
    String format_for_html_display()

interface StockWebConglomerator
    CustomWebPage find_by_ticker(Ticker)
    CustomWebPage find_by_name(CompanyName)
```

With this approach, the generalization of WebConglomerator to cover other types of information is in the reuse of the framework—the pattern of the interfaces involved—rather than attempting to create a universal WebConglomerator.

You could generalize these interfaces using a language-specific generic mechanism. For example, a more general interface might be coded with a template, as follows:[10]

```
template <Type>
interface InformationTransformer
            {
            gather_data(Type key);
            String format_for_html_display();
            }
    interface WebConglomerator
            {
            CustomWebPage find(Type key);
            }
```

9.8 Things to Remember

The Web Conglomerator demonstrated a number of points to keep in mind:

---

[10]Developing this generic interface suggests that the Finder methods should be called outside of the WebConglomerator. We leave that alteration to the reader.

- Construct tests for interfaces as you create the interfaces.

- Create functional tests that are implementation independent.

- Separate information retrieval from information display.

The system also showed when developing interfaces that may be useful in a variety of contexts, you can:

- Create a concrete implementation of an interface before abstracting it.

- Develop application specific interfaces before generalizing them.

- Generalize interfaces using frameworks or templates

Chapter 10

Service Registry

In Chapter 5 on remote interfaces, we discussed looking up service providers for an interface in a directory. In this chapter, we're going to create a general service registry as a means for exploring some issues in providing networked services. This registry also will give us an opportunity to experience a document-style interface.

10.1 Vision

The Service Registry allows users to advertise the availability of service providers, even if their computers do not have static Internet Protocol (IP) addresses.

The services do not have to be on reserved ports, such as the HTTP port (80), or use any particular protocol, such as SOAP or RMI. A couple of examples demonstrate how the Service Registry will work.

Suppose you have a video camera connected to your computer in your house. Your computer connects to the Internet via a dynamically assigned IP address.[1] Since the IP address is dynamic, you need some way to discover it. The Service Registry provides that ability.

The program connected to your camera registers a service identifier (a ServiceID), an IP address, and a port with the Service Registry. You are sitting at work and want to see the picture on your web cam. On

---

[1] Dynamic addresses tend to be the same for long periods of time. Suppose you want to look at the video from the camera on other computers, such as the one in your office. You might note the IP address before you left the house. The address may be the same when you attempt to connect. However, in general, you should not rely on a "static" dynamic IP address.

IP Addresses and Ports

The Domain Name System (DNS) supplies IP addresses (e.g., 66.15.240.233) for host names (e.g., www.pughkilleen.com).* The IP address is usually the same for long periods of time (static). A dynamic DNS address provides a way to connect to computers that do not have static IP addresses, such as those connected via cable, DSL, or phone lines. Dynamic DNS's are updated frequently with new addresses.

Servers, such as a web server, communicate over a port. You can think of a port as the equivalent to the number of a phone extension. To communicate with a server, you need to know on what port it is communicating. Standard services, such as web servers, have fixed port numbers. For example, web servers communicate on port 80 and mail servers on port 25.

Nonstandard services may communicate on any port. DNS (normal or dynamic) provides only IP addresses. So, it's harder to provide nonstandard services that do not have fixed port numbers.[†]

---

*See http://en.wikipedia.org/wiki/Dns for more information.
[†]Remote Procedure Calls (RPCs) have a separate mechanism (e.g., Unix's RPC Mapper) that runs on each host for providing port numbers for services. Java's JINI provides a Java language version of a combined IP address/port number lookup.

your office computer, the program that displays the video looks up the ServiceID in the Service Registry, retrieves the IP address and port, and then connects to the program on your home computer.

As another example, suppose you are developing a new interactive game that involves communication between two or more players. The players install your software on their computers and want to link up. Unless they are using fixed IP addresses with fixed port assignments, they will have to manually communicate to each other their current IP addresses and ports.

When your game program starts up on each player's computer, it sends to the Service Registry your game's ServiceID and the IP address and port that the game program has been assigned by the operating system. Your game also looks up on the Service Registry any current registered providers for your game's ServiceID. It can use the retrieved IP

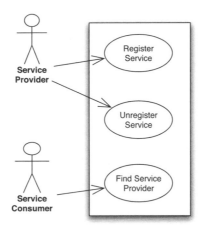

Figure 10.1: USE CASES

addresses and ports to talk to the other currently registered game programs. When your game program exits, it tells the Service Registry to remove its registration.

10.2 Conceptualization

We come up with three use cases for this system, as shown in Figure Figure 10.1.

To simplify the descriptions of the use cases, let's create an abstraction:

- ServiceProviderInformation

    - ServiceID identifies the service.

    - ConnectionInformation identifies the means to connect, e.g., IP address, protocol, and port.

The Service Registry does not specify the protocol to be used between the provider of a service (a ServiceProvider) and the user of that service (a ServiceConsumer). The protocol could be anything from simple text transfer to SOAP to binary data, such as video. The person creating the ServiceProvider for a ServiceID is responsible for determining the desired protocol and placing the appropriate values into ConnectionInformation. We made ConnectionInformation more abstract so that it applies to any type of connection, such as a phone number, a mail address, or a GPS location. But following the "get something working" guideline, we will limit the implementation to Internet connections.

Here are informal descriptions of each use case:

 Use Case: Register Service

1. ServiceProvider sends ServiceProviderInformation.

2. Server registers ServiceProviderInformation.

 Use Case: Unregister Service

1. ServiceProvider sends ServiceProviderInformation.

2. Server unregisters ServiceProviderInformation.

 Use Case: Find Service Provider

1. ServiceConsumer sends ServiceID

2. If ServiceProviderInformation with matching ServiceID is registered,

   Server returns ConnectionInformation

   else

   Server signals ServiceIDNotFound.

10.3 Analysis

The IRI cards we created are shown in Figure 10.2, on the facing page. Since the use cases are simple, the cards turn out to also be simple. The Service Registry has all the responsibilities.

We work through the use cases to see whether we have captured all the essential features. For Register Service, the ServiceProvider sends ServiceProviderInformation to the registry. The registry stores that information. For Unregister Service, the ServiceProvider also sends the ServiceInformation to the registry, and the registry removes it from storage.

In Find Service Provider, a ServiceConsumer requests the ConnectionInformation for a ServiceProvider by providing a ServiceID. The registry returns either the ConnectionInformation for a ServiceProvider or an indication that no associated ServiceProvider exists.

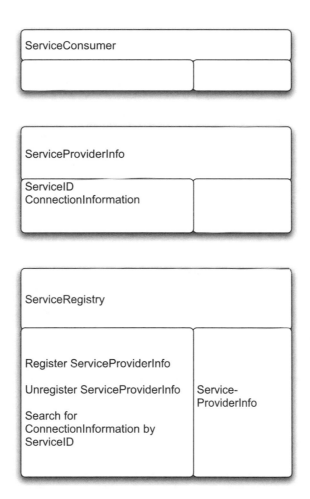

Figure 10.2: SERVICE REGISTRY IRI CARDS

Working through the use cases with these cards provides no additional insights, so we start developing tests for this system.

Unique ServiceIDs

We're not registering users for the Service Registry. Anyone can use the system. How can we ensure that each service uses a unique ServiceID? We can use a universal unique identifier (UUID) to identify the service and the servers.[2] A UUID can be generated on almost any computer and is practically guaranteed to be unique. No central registration is required to guarantee this uniqueness. The UUID is 128-bits long and is typically expressed as a 36-character string (with some hyphens).

Testing Registration

We come up with the tests that follow. Once again, the use cases are simple, so the functional tests are simple.

Test Case: Simple Registration and Lookup

1. Register a ServiceProvider.

2. Look up ServiceID—it should succeed.

Test Case: Registration, Deregistration and Lookup

1. Register ServiceProvider.

2. Unregister that ServiceProvider.

3. Look up a ServiceID—should signal ServiceIDNotFound.

Test Case: No Registration and Lookup

1. Look up ServiceID for unregistered service—it should signal ServiceIDNotFound.

---

[2]This is a GUID to you Microsoft folks. A UUID can use an Ethernet address and the time of day to generate a unique identifier. Ethernet addresses are usually unique, unless two administrators set an updatable Ethernet address to the same value. Another version of UUID uses a random number generator to create a unique identifier.

Test Case: Two Service Providers

1. Register a ServiceProvider.

2. Register a second ServiceProvider.

3. Look up a ServiceID—should return two ConnectionInformations.

4. Unregister first ServiceProvider.

5. Look up a ServiceID—should return ConnectionInformation for second ServiceProvider

6. Unregister second ServiceProvider

7. Look up a ServiceID—should return ServiceIDNotFound

We probably want to try some variations of Two Service Providers test, such as unregistering the second and registering it again. To further help understand the system we are developing, we create some misuse tests:

Test Case: Double Registration and Lookup

1. Register a ServiceProvider with some values for ConnectionInformation

2. Register same ServiceProvider again (without unregistering) with different values for ConnectionInformation

3. Look up ServiceID—what should it return?

Tests can clarify the contract (see Chapter 2) that a ServiceProvider has with a ServiceRegistry. In the Double Registration and Lookup test, a ServiceProvider fails to unregister itself. When the same ServiceProvider next registers, it may have different connection information. How does the ServiceRegistry know which ServiceProvider to overwrite? Even if there were only one entry, it's possible that another ServiceProvider registered it. It appears we need to add a ServiceProviderID to the ServiceProviderInformation block. That way, we know definitively which entry to replace if the same ServiceProvider registers twice for the same ServiceID without unregistering. It appears this change is easy to implement—we can look up current ServiceProviders either by a ServiceProviderID or by ConnectionInformation.

Unregistration

Another issue comes up with the failure to unregister. It's possible that a ServiceProvider never unregisters and never contacts the ServiceRegistry again. Suppose the computer that provides the service is a laptop. The owner walks into a wireless access point, starts the computer, and registers the service. Then he closes up the laptop without unregistering and walks out. The entry is still in the registry. The entry would become stale and take up space.

For potential solutions to this problem, we can look for analogies in other systems. The DNS has a TimeToLive field that describes how long an entry should be kept in a cache. Following along those lines, we can add a TimeToLive to the ServiceProviderInformation. The ServiceRegistry can periodically clean itself by discarding entries that died long ago, or it can delete dead entries it finds when searching for a service. The addition of TimeToLive requires that ServiceProviders reregister themselves periodically (i.e., before the TimeToLive expires). We'll program our first iteration without this feature, as well-behaved ServiceProviders do not require it. We note that the feature should be implemented in a future iteration.

Testing Performance

The next test checks to see how well the ServiceRegistry reacts to a large number of ServiceProviders. This can be used as both a capacity performance test and a speed performance test.

 Test Case: Multiple Service Providers

1. Register many ServiceProviders.

2. Look up ServiceID should return equal number of ConnectionInformations.

3. Repeat this sequence with random registration and deregistration for ServiceProviders, and see whether numbers and ServiceProviders agree with expectations.

The Multiple Service Providers test brings up an interesting issue. If a service was popular, there may be hundreds, if not thousands, of ServiceProviders for that service. Responding to a request by a ServiceConsumer for that service may yield a very long result. We could place a limit on the number of ServiceProviders that are registered for a particular ServiceID. Or we could limit the number of ConnectionInformations that are returned for a request. At this point, the rule of "get something working" applies here. We note this issue in our design notebook so we can deal with it latter.

Security

Since this service can be used by anyone in the outside world, we need to play close attention to security. Typically, frameworks such as J2EE provide security with user authentication (e.g., username/password) and authorization (e.g., access controls). But in this case, we are not requiring any logon, so we'll need to incorporate some security mechanisms in the system. A full-fledged risk assessment is beyond the scope of this book, so we'll just take a brief look.[3] Let's consider some security issues that may affect our design.

This service does not provide authentication of a ServiceProvider. The ServiceRegistry can ensure only that the IP address in the ConnectionInformation matches the IP address that is used to register the ServiceProvider. It's possible that a ServiceProvider registers a server for a ServiceID that works like a Trojan (the server appears to offer the real service, but it's really something else). If security is an issue, then the ServiceConsumer needs to verify the ServiceProvider's identity by a mechanism external to this registry. We need to make clear to our users that the contract (see Chapter 2) of ServiceRegistry does not include authentication.

For example, suppose each copy of a multiplayer game program registers itself as a ServiceProvider. Each game program retrieves the other ServiceProviders. The programs can interact and provide identification that gives a relative level of certainty that each is a legitimate game program. The game program might have registration keys or digital certificates that are interchanged, and each game could check the validity of the other's registration keys.

A ServiceConsumer may try to find a service to which they should not be allowed to connect. We could leave it up to the ServiceProvider to authenticate a ServiceConsumer. For example, the ServiceConsumer could provide a password directly to a ServiceProvider to authenticate itself. On the other hand, the RegistryService might provide one more level of security by having the ServiceProvider submit a password. ServiceConsumers

---

[3]See *Software Security: Building Security In* by Gary McGraw (Addison-Wesley Professional, 2006) for a full discussion of security.

would have to submit a password value that matches the ServicerProvider password before the registry returns the ConnectionInformation for a particular ServiceProvider. That way, a ServiceConsumer would not be able to easily learn the location of a ServiceProvider. We acknowledge the potential need for this feature but place it in a future iteration. The addition will have some effect on the communication, so we need to ensure a way of transitioning (see "Versioning" in Chapter 6).

We could check that unregistration for a ServiceProvider came from the IP address in the ConnectionInformation. However, that would not allow a ServiceProvider that switched IP addresses to remove the previous entry. If we permitted unregistration from a different IP, a hacker could try to unregister a ServiceProvider, if they knew the ServiceProviderID. We'll make sure that the ServiceProviderID is not sent to a ServiceConsumer, so the hacker would need to try many values for ServiceProviderID. These attempts would probably show up as a Denial of Service (DOS) attack.

A DOS attack is a major concern. Registrations or lookups could be sent at a rate that could overwhelm the server. If the requests were all coming from the same IP address, then you can easily deny multiple connections or repetitive connections from that IP address. You could limit requests from an IP address to a reasonable number (e.g., one per second). Requests after a certain number during a period might be refused. However, this defense will not prevent distributed attacks that come from multiple IP addresses. A firewall can provide some protection against DOS attacks. However, we may want to add internal protection if we are running this system on a host not protected by a firewall that we can control or just as a second layer of defense. In our initial iteration, we let the firewall have full responsibility for handling DOS attacks. That simplifies our development.

We should be concerned about eavesdropping on communication between the registry server and the clients. To protect the communications, we can use the underlying security of web connections for protection, such as the encryption in the Secure Socket Layer (SSL). For our original development we can use unencrypted communication. We should be attentive in developing the interfaces to ensure that the type of communication (unencrypted or encrypted) is opaque.

We put the password, DOS, and encryption issues onto the feature lists to be addressed in future iterations.

10.4   Design

We have two parts to design: the remote client and the ServiceRegistry server. Let's first work on the communication between the two. We will use document-style interfaces (see Chapter 6) to communicate between the two systems. This style allows communication between different types of platforms and languages.

The Document Interface

With this service registry, the documents match the three actions: register, unregister, and lookup. The documents contain a common element, ServiceProviderInformation:

```
Data: ServiceProviderInformation
    ServiceID
    ConnectionInformation
    ServiceProviderID

Document: Registration
    Version
    ServiceProviderInformation

Document: RegistrationResponse
    Version
    Status // Success or failure

Document: Unregistration
    Version
    ServiceProviderInformation

Document: LookupRequest
    Version
    ServiceID

Document: LookupResponse
    Version
    ServiceID
    ConnectionInformation []
```

We added a Version to each document. We know we have potential changes, but we don't know whether or when we are going to make those changes. The version identifier allows both the server and the client to easily distinguish between the current and older versions.

The document flow (interface protocol) appears in Figure 10.3, on the next page.

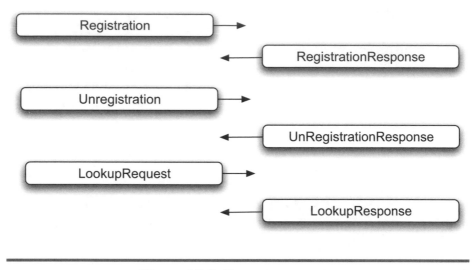

Figure 10.3: DOCUMENT FLOW

Since we are not in control of the code the ServiceProvider uses for submittal, the server should validate the document before further processing it. These documents do not have much data to validate. The Version should be a recognized one. The ServiceProviderID, ServiceID, and ConnectionInformation should follow a prescribed format.

We figured out the information we need to convey in the documents, but we haven't specified the format. We also haven't specified the format that will be used to transmit and receive the documents. Our document flow should be independent of the format and protocol, as discussed in Chapter 6. In the next section, we'll create an interface to these documents to simplify their use.

10.5 Implementation

We'll create an interface to demonstrate the issues with which a client may have to deal. We'd also like to provide an interface for the clients so they do not need to code each element in the document interface. This keeps the format of transmission more opaque.

Interfaces to the Document

Let's first create an interface for the documents that are going to be interchanged. These represent DTOs (see Chapter 6) that are derived from the document structure previously presented. Each of these DTOs can validate as much as possible the information that is placed into it (e.g., the UUID contains the correct number of characters), as well as transform itself to and from the external format.

```
data interface ServiceProviderInformation
    UUID service_id
    ConnectionInformation connection_information
    UUID service_provider_id

data interface Registration
    Version the_version
    ServiceProviderInformation provider_information

enumeration StatusValue {Success, Failure, Warning}
data interface RegistrationResponse
    Version the_version
    Status StatusValue
    String status_explanation

data interface Unregistration
    Version the_version
    ServiceProviderInformation provider_information

data interface UnRegistrationResponse
    Version the_version
    Status StatusValue
    String status_explanation

data interface LookupRequest
    Version the_version
    UUID service_id

data interface LookupResponse
    Version the_version
    uuid service_id
    ConnectionInformation [] connections
```

A ServiceRegistry client constructs the documents, sends them to the server, and interprets the response. We can add higher-level procedural interfaces that perform these operations. The interfaces for the two kinds of ServiceRegistry users might look like this:

```
interface ServiceConsumer
    ConnectionInformation [] lookup_service(UUID service_id)
        signals UnableToConnect, NoServiceProviders

interface ServiceProvider
    register_service(UUID service_id, UUID server_id,
        ConnectionInformation connect_info)  signals UnableToConnect,
            RegistrationFailure,
```

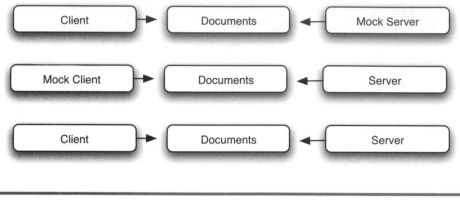

Figure 10.4: TESTS

```
unregister_service(UUID service_id, UUID server_id,
    ConnectionInformation connect_info) signals UnableToConnect,
    UnRegistrationFailure
```

The implementation of each of these interfaces may fail to connect to the server. If so, they signal UnableToConnect. We'll leave it up to the client to determine what to do in that situation. They may try again or immediately notify the user of the failure. These interfaces need to implement the flow of the document protocol as shown in Figure 10.3, on page 172.

Using these two interfaces, we code the tests we created in the analysis section. To test the client, we can create a mock server that returns a response appropriate to the request. To test the server, we can create a set of documents using the DTOs, send them to the server, and then check the response documents. To test the system as a whole, the client sends the documents to the server. See Figure 10.4.

Document Format Details

The selection of the document format should affect only the code that translates to the external format and from the external. We could use almost any form of communication between the client and the server (e.g., web services, HTTP, etc.). The considerations for picking a format include choosing one that is easy to parse and fairly standard.

Code

The full code for the client interfaces and the document interfaces is on the web site listed in the preface. To show how the interfaces interact, here is the code in Java for the two types of clients. The code transforms the document-style interface into a procedural-style interface.

```java
public class ServiceProviderImplementation implements ServiceProvider
    {
    public void registerService(UUID serviceID, UUID serverID,
        ConnectionInformation connectInfo)
        throws UnableToConnectException, BadFormatException,
        UnableToRegisterException
        {
        ServiceProviderInformation spi = new ServiceProviderInformation(
            serviceID, serverID, connectInfo);
        RegistrationDocument registration = new RegistrationDocument(spi);
        RegistrationResponseDocument response =
            (RegistrationResponseDocument)
                RegistryConnection.getResponseDocument(
                Configuration.getRegistryDomain(), registration);
        if (!response.getStatus())
            {
            throw new UnableToRegisterException();
            }
        return ;
        }

    public void unregisterService(UUID serviceId, UUID serverId,
            ConnectionInformation connectInfo)
        // Looks the same, except the document are for unregistration
}
```

Here is the code for a ServiceConsumer implementation:

```java
public class ServiceConsumerImplementation implements ServiceConsumer
    {
    public ConnectionInformation[] lookupService(UUID serviceID)
        throws UnableToConnectException, BadFormatException,
        NoServiceProviders
        {
        LookupRequestDocument lookupRequest =
            new LookupRequestDocument(serviceID);
        LookupResponseDocument lookupResponse =
            (LookupResponseDocument) RegistryConnection
            .getResponseDocument( Configuration.getRegistryDomain(),
            lookupRequest);
        if (lookupResponse.getConnectionInformation().length == 0)
            throw new NoServiceProviders();
        return lookupResponse.getConnectionInformation();
        }
    }
```

10.6 Published Interface

This is going to be a "published interface" (see Chapter 6). So before we start distributing the document interface specifications, we ought to consider how the interface might change in the future. If we can anticipate some of the changes, based on knowledge of other systems or past experience, we may avoid some messy redoing of the interface. We cannot anticipate everything, but if we've seen the situation before, we ought to consider the consequences.

We've previously looked at some of the changes in the documents themselves that might be required for security. The two issues we'll now look at concern making the system more resilient to failure and making it more scalable. The design of any system that provides remote interfaces needs to address these two facets. Issues here may affect the flow of documents, not just the contents of the documents.

Multiple Servers

In a real-life system, a single server is a single point of failure for the system. If that server fails, no one can use the service. We should have multiple servers. The ServiceProvider and ServiceConsumer interfaces we outlined in the previous section are not going to change. But either the server is going to become more complicated or the underlying code for these client interfaces is going to have to handle multiple servers.

We could use the master/slave form of backup that the DNS uses. One server acts as the master for the information. The slaves periodically contact the master for new information. However, with the DNS the information changes infrequently. The information for a new domain or a new mail server may take a bit of time (up to 24 hours) to disseminate. With the ServiceRegistry, entries are constantly being updated, so using the same structure would necessitate a lot of communication between servers.

We make a simple decision. The ServiceProvider is responsible for contacting multiple servers. Each registry server will think it is the only server. For retrieval, a ServiceConsumer needs to contact one server. If that server goes down or does not have a ServiceProvider entry, it can contact another server.

Let's give an example. Suppose we have three servers at the following addresses:

```
mainserver1.1020.net
mainserver2.1020.net
mainserver3.1020.net
```

The ServiceProvider contacts all three of these servers and registers/un-registers on all three. If it cannot contact any of them, then an Unable-ToConnect signal is generated.

On the other hand, a ServiceConsumer starts by contacting one of these servers. If it cannot reach the first server, it contacts one of the other ones. It reports UnableToConnect only if all servers are not available. If it cannot find a ServiceProvider entry on any of the servers, it returns NoServiceProviders.[4]

Distributed Servers

We expect that the system will attract a number of people who want to use it as a directory service. One server will not be able to handle Server-ProviderInformations for the entire universe. We need to have additional servers for handling some of the work and a mechanism for distributing the work. Once again, we turn to the existing DNS for a model on how to distribute servers.[5] A program looks up a domain name in the DNS by first contacting a "root" server. A number of root servers provide redundancy. The root server responds with the names of servers that may have the detailed information for a particular domain. The program then contacts one of those servers to see whether it has the details. That server can respond with either the IP addresses for names or other servers that actually have the addresses.

To create an analogy of that flow, we can add two document types: Ser-viceIDServerLookupRequest and ServerIDServerLookupResponse. They look like this:

```
Document: ServiceIDServerLookupRequest
    Version
    ServiceID
Document: ServerIDServerLookupResponse
    Version
    ServiceID
    ConnectionInformation []
```

---

[4]There is a possible situation where a ServiceProvider can connect to some of the servers, but the ServiceConsumers can connect only to the others. What to do? Luckily, we did not make any guarantees as to performance, so we can simply say, "Sorry."

[5]This is a simplified version of how the DNS works. For more information, see http://en.wikipedia.org/wiki/DNS.

These documents look practically the same as LookupRequest and Lookup-Response. The difference is that the requested service is one defined by the registry itself, rather than by an end user. Before registering or looking up a ServiceID, the client makes a ServiceIDServerLookupRequest to determine which server to contact.

A ServiceProvider would always send ServiceIDServerLookupRequest. We might require a ServiceConsumer also to send it, or we could return two different documents (LookupResponse and ServerIDServerLookupResponse) to a LookupRequest. The ServiceConsumer would need to distinguish between the two responses to see whether it needed to perform another lookup. In either case, the procedural ServiceConsumer interface does not change. Its implementation just becomes a little more complicated. Having LookupRequest return two different responses cuts down on the number of documents that need to be transmitted, at a slight complication of handling two different response documents.

Even though we have only a single server for the moment, we should consider the changes to the document interface that might be required if we need to expand to distributed servers. We will develop our first iteration without multiple servers and deploy it to a small number of test users. Before publishing the interface to a larger audience, we will want to add the distributed service messages. The changes are not just additions to existing documents, but rather reflect a change in the document protocol.

Implementation

This following code implements multiple servers for a ServiceConsumer. Note that the method interface is the same for the single version. When accessing multiple implementations, you need to handle the exceptions from each individual service. In this case, an exception is returned only if all implementations produced that exception.

```
public ConnectionInformation[] lookupService(UUID serviceID)
    throws UnableToConnectException, BadFormatException,
    NoServiceProviders
    {
    ServiceIDServerLookupRequestDocument lookupRequest =
        new ServiceIDServerLookupRequestDocument(
        serviceID);
    ConnectionInformation[] servers = lookupServers(
        Configuration.getRegistryDomain(), serviceID);
    if (servers.length == 0)
        throw new NoServiceProviders();
```

```
int countUnableToConnect = 0;
int countBadFormat = 0;
int countNoServiceProviders = 0;
for (int i = 0; i < servers.length; i++)
    {
    try
        {
        ConnectionInformation[] connInfo =
            lookupService(servers[i].toString(), serviceID);
        return connInfo;
        }
    catch (UnableToConnectException e)
        { countUnableToConnect++;}
    catch (BadFormatException e)
        { countBadFormat++;}
    catch (NoServiceProviders e)
        { countNoServiceProviders++;}
    }
if (countUnableToConnect == servers.length)
    throw new UnableToConnectException();
if (countBadFormat == servers.length)
    throw new BadFormatException("Bad format");
if (countNoServiceProviders -- servers.length)
    throw new NoServiceProviders();
return new ConnectionInformation[0];
}
```

10.7 The Next Iterations

Software should be developed in incremental iterations; you'll have the
joy of a working system at the end of each iteration, rather than waiting
years to see something happening. During each iteration, you may
discover new insights into a system—this applies both to developers
and to end users.

We have our basic ServiceRegistry working. It's time to add a few features
and see how they will affect the published interface. We'd like to be able
to gracefully change the interface without requiring users of older versions to make changes. We'll add TimeToLive to ServiceProviderInformation,
as previously discussed in this chapter. We'll also add authorization for
ServiceProviders/ServiceConsumers, which we considered in the first iteration. We delayed implementing these features, as we wanted to make
sure our minimum feature set was working.

TimeToLive

When we add TimeToLive to ServiceProviderInformation, the data in Service-ProviderInformation changes. Since we used a version identifier, as shown in Chapter 6, we increase that value. In the server, we need to check the version in the incoming document against that value. If the incoming document is an earlier version, we need to set a default value for the missing TimeToLive.

Now we have an example of a common trade-off to make in updating a document protocol. Should the default value be more restrictive or less restrictive? In this example, should we default TimeToLive to be a long time or a short time? What did we specify in the original interface contract? We stated through the document protocol that a registration terminated when it was unregistered. However, we did not specify the length of time a registration could be present.

We could default TimeToLive to a large time to make it correspond to our implicit contract. If we default to a short time, we need to communicate with our users that the contract has changed, in the spirit of the First Law of Interfaces. We can make a change in our client contract by adding a Warning. If the status of a response is Warning, the client should probably notify the user with a message.

We could put TimeToLive either in ServiceProviderInformation or in Registration. You can decide based on which data TimeToLive seems more cohesive (Chapter 4). Is it closer associated with a registration itself or the information contained within? It's a toss-up in this case, since there is only one set of information provided within the registration. We'll make it part of ServiceProviderInformation:

```
Data: ServiceProviderInformation
    ServiceID
    ConnectionInformation
    ServiceProviderID
    TimeToLIve

Document: Registration
    Version
    ServiceProviderInformation
```

The tests involved for this change include the following:

- Making a registration with a short TimeToLive and checking that the information is not returned after that time

- Making a registration with an older version and seeing whether a Warning is received

ServiceConsumer Authorization

As we noted previously, a ServiceProvider may want to provide a service only to selected ServiceConsumers. You would not want everybody in the world to be able to access your home video. So, we can add authorization information (e.g., a password). We will provide ConnectionInformation to a ServiceConsumer only if they supply authorization information matching that supplied by the ServiceProvider.

The document interface changes are as follows:

```
Data: ServiceProviderInformation
    ServiceID
    ConnectionInformation
    ServiceProviderID
    TimeToLive
    Authorization

Document: LookupRequest
    Version
    ServiceID
    Authorization
```

If a ServiceProvider does not require authorization, the Authorization is blank (zero-length string). Otherwise, the ServiceRegistry server returns ConnectionInformation only for the ServiceProviderInformation entries whose Authorization matches the Authorization in the LookupRequest.

This additional data item does not require a substantial change in the contract. It's clear that the default for Authorization should be blank for an older document that does not contain an Authorization field. If a ServiceProvider decides that it wants to start using authorization, it needs to upgrade to the new version of the interface. Each corresponding ServiceConsumer also needs to upgrade.[6]

The tests involved for this change include the following:

- Making a registration with a blank Authorization and checking to see whether it is returned for a service lookup

---

[6]In addition, the users of ServiceProvider need to contact the users of each ServiceConsumer to give them the password. That communication occurs outside of the ServiceRegistry system.

So, How Do We Get a ServiceID?

You may be wondering how a ServiceConsumer determines what ServiceID to look for. If the ServiceConsumer is part of a distributed program, the author of that program provides the ServiceID. If not, other systems already in place can provide the means to discover what is the ServiceID for a particular service. For example, a service provider can send an email with the ServiceID to anybody who's interested in using that service. They could place the ServiceID on a web page along with enough contextual information that it could be found with a Google search. For example, the page could contain this:

```
ServiceName1020: Texas Hold'Em Poker Players
ServiceUUID1020: c8b522d1-5cf3-11ce-ade5-00aa0044773e
ServiceDescription1020:  This service identifies players
    who want to play Texas Hold'Em.
```

You could create a program that performs a search for services and return the ServiceID. The program could be based on the ideas in the Web Conglomerator in Chapter 9.

- Making a registration with a value in Authorization, and making a service lookup with a blank Authorization and checking to see that the corresponding registration is not returned for a service lookup

- Making a registration with a value in Authorization, and making a service lookup with the same value in Authorization and checking to see that the corresponding registration is returned for a service lookup

10.8 Things to Remember

We explored a specific example of using remote document-style interfaces. Along the way, we saw how to:

- Examine the initial interface before publishing.

- Plan for document versioning.

- Create a procedural-style interface for a document-style interface.

- Create tests to understand how the document flow should handle errors.

We investigated some issues with remote interface providers such as the service directory:

- Explore security considerations starting in the initial design.

- Consider how the client should react to connection or server failures

- Determine how to handle server redundancy.

Chapter 11

Patterns

11.1 Introduction

We introduced some patterns in the previous chapters. In this chapter,
we'll review those patterns and cover a few patterns that revolve pri-
marily around the substitutability of different implementations. Using
common patterns can make your design more understandable to other
developers.

Each pattern has trade-offs. The "Gang of Four" book[1] details the trade-
offs. In this chapter, we list some of the prominent trade-offs.

11.2 Factory Method

The Factory Method pattern is the quintessential way to obtain an
implementation of an interface. You call a method that returns a reference to an implementation. With a factory method, you can easily substitute implementations without having to change a single line of code
in the calling method. Let's take the example of the WebPageParser. In
the code that uses the method, we could create an instance of a particular parser. For example:

```
class RegularExpressionWebPageParser implements WebPageParser
    {// some code} .
WebPageParser web_page_parser  = new RegularExpressionWebPageParser();
```

From that point onward in the code, we really don't care what the
implementation is for WebPageParser. However, if we want to change

---

[1] *Design Patterns* by Gamma, et al

the implementation, we have to alter the type of object we are creating. Instead, we can use a factory method to create a WebPageParser:[2]

```
class WebPageParserFactory
    static WebPageParser get_web_page_parser()

// Use of method
WebPageParser web_page_parser =
    WebPageParserFactory.get_web_page_parser();
```

Now we can change the implementing class in a single place, and all users will get the new implementation.

We could make the factory method a little more intelligent and specify some criteria for choosing a particular parser. We might want a fast but possibly inaccurate parser or a meticulous one that can parse anything. We do not need to specify a particular name, just our needs. For example:

```
WebPageParser web_page_parser =
    WebPageParserFactory.get_web_page_parser(SLOW_BUT_METICULOUS);
```

A registry lookup works like the Factory Method pattern. You request an implementation of an interface using a service identifier. The method call is a little more generic. For example:

```
WebPageParser web_page_parser =
    (WebPageParser) registry.lookup(WebPageParserID)
```

The Abstract Factory pattern works one more level up from a Factory Method pattern. You may have multiple interfaces, and for each one you want to create related implementations. In the Service Registry example in Chapter 10, we had several different documents. The representation of these documents could be in XML, YAML, tab-delimited text, or another format. We could provide implementations for each document that encoded the data in a particular representation. For example:

```
interface RegistrationDocument
    set_version()
    set_service_provider_information()
interface LookupResponseDocument
    set_version()
    set_service_id()
    set_connection_information()
```

---

[2]We show this as static, which makes get_web_page_parser() a class method. Otherwise, we would have to create or find an implementation of WebPageParserFactory before we can get a WebPageParser.

```
interface DocumentFactory
    RegistrationDocument get_registration_document()
    LookupResponseDocument get_lookup_response_document()
```

Now you create multiple implementations of DocumentFactory. Each version of DocumentFactory creates RegistrationDocuments and LookupResponseDocuments that encode information in a particular format.

FACTORY METHOD

> Advantage—makes implementation of interface transparent

ABSTRACT FACTORY

> Advantage—makes implementation of set of interfaces transparent

11.3 Proxy

In the Proxy pattern, you have multiple implementations of a single interface. One implementation (the proxy) acts as an intermediary to another implementation. Each method in the proxy may perform some internal operations and then call the corresponding method in another implementation. The implementations may be in the same program, in the same computer, in different processes, or in different computers.

The caller of a proxy usually need not be aware that the proxy being called is making calls to other implementations. The functions that proxies can perform include security, caching of results, and synchronization[3] A common use of a proxy is to provide a local interface to a remote interface. This is termed a *remote proxy*. For example, here's an interface to get the current price for a stock:

```
interface StockTickerQuoter
    Dollar get_current_price(Ticker)
```

You can get a local copy by using either a specific class or a factory method, as in the previous section. For example:

```
StockTickerQuoter stock_ticker_quoter =
    new StockTickerQuoterLocalImplementation()
```

The local implementation connects to a remote implementation via a network connection, typically a Remote Procedure Call (see Chapter 6).

---

[3]See http://www.research.umbc.edu/~tarr/dp/lectures/Proxy-2pp.pdf for more details.

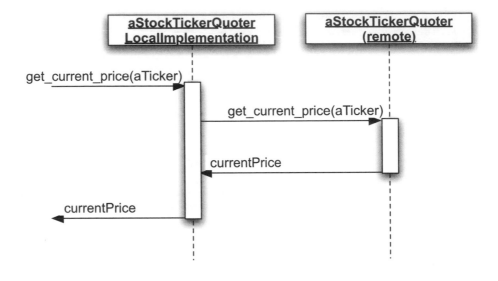

Figure 11.1: CONNECTION SEQUENCE

The remote implementation has exactly the same interface. Figure 11.1 shows the sequence diagram.

The same interface might be used with multiple proxies that perform various services. The services could include security checking, encryption/decryption, and logging.[4] If we want these services to be dynamically added, typically the interface includes a way to denote another proxy in the chain. For example, we could log each time a price was requested by adding another implementation in the chain:

```
interface StockTickerQuoter
    Dollar get_current_price(Ticker)
    set_next_stock_ticker_quoter(StockTickerQuoter);
class StockTickerQuoterLogger implements StockTickerQuoter
    {
    StockTickerQuoter next_stock_ticker_quoter;
    set_next_stock_ticker_quoter(StockTickerQuoter stq)
        {
        next_stock_ticker_quoter = stq;
        }
```

_____

[4]Some authors suggest that these additional services would make this a Decorator pattern (see the next section).

```
Dollar get_current_price(Ticker a_ticker)
    {
    Logger.send_message("Another quote");
    return next_stock_ticker_quoter.
        get_current_price(Ticker a_ticker)
    }
}
```

Now we can give the original implementation of the interface another implementation to invoke:

```
StockTickerQuoter stock_ticker_quoter =
    new StockTickerQuoterLogger();
stock_ticker_quoter.set_next_stock_ticker_quoter
    (new StockTickerQuoterLocalImplementation());
```

(Some authors consider this a variation of the Decorator pattern, which is discussed next. They suggest that the StockTickerQuoterCounter decorates another StockTickerQuoter by adding a logging functionality.)

When we get a current price, the price is not only retrieved, but a message is also logged. After the initial setup, the use of StockTickerQuoter in the remainder of the program does not change.

PROXY

> Advantage—additional features (security, logging, etc.) can be added transparently.

11.4 Decorator

The Decorator pattern works like the Proxy pattern. The decorator has the same interface as the decorated interface. Typically, it also has an additional interface that represents the decoration. In the previous Proxy pattern example, the user might not be aware that StockTickerQuoterLogger was part of the proxy chain.

On the other hand, the user typically is the one decorating a class. For example, we might add a feature that counts the number of times we asked for a stock quote. This feature is provided by an additional interface, Counter. The decorator implements this interface as well as the original one. For each method in the original interface, it may just call the one in the decorated implementation, or it may add some functionality. For example:

```
interface Counter
    {
    int get_count();
```

```
        reset_count()
    }
class StockTickerQuoterCounter implements StockTickerQuoter, Counter
    {
    int counter;
    int get_count()
        {
        return counter;
    }
    void reset_count()
        {
        counter = 0;
    }
    StockTickerQuoter next_stock_ticker_quoter;
    set_next_stock_ticker_quoter(StockTickerQuoter stq)
        {
        next_stock_ticker_quoter = stq;
    }
     Dollar get_current_price(Ticker a_ticker)
        {
        counter++;
        return next_stock_ticker_quoter.
            get_current_price(Ticker a_ticker)
    }
    }
```

The get_current_price() method delegates to another implementation. In addition, it increments a count that is accessible by the Counter interface. When we're using this class, we give it an implementation to decorate:

```
StockTickerQuoterCounter stock_ticker_quoter_decorator =
    new StockTickerQuoterCounter();
stock_ticker_quoter_decorator.set_next_stock_ticker_quoter
    (new StockTickerQuoterLocalImplementation());
```

This code looks a lot like the proxy version. The difference is that you can call additional methods on stock_ticker_quoter_decorator, such as get_count(). Another difference is that proxies are often designed to work together. The Decorator pattern can be used on classes that existed before the decorator is created.

DECORATOR

Advantage—adds behavior on classes not explicitly designed for expansion

11.5 Adapter

Adaptation is a major feature of interface-oriented design. You create the interface you need. If a module exists whose interface is close to your need, you can alter your interface to match that existing interface. Otherwise, you can adapt the interface of that module to match your desired interface. For example, in the Link Checker, we created a WebPageParser interface:

```
interface WebPageParser
    URL [] parse_for_URLs(WebPage)
```

Java has an HTMLParser that performs the services needed by a realization of this interface. It has different method names. So, we create an adapter that implements the WebPageParser interface by using the HTMLParser class.

An implementation of WebPageParser can adapt different interface styles to the style represented by WebPageParser. For example, WebPageParser uses a pull style. You ask it for a set of links after it parses the document. You could create an implementation that employs the push style, such as the SAX parser. Internal methods would gather the links into a collection, and parse_for_URLs() would return that collection.

The interface an existing class provides may not meet the paradigm that you want for your classes. So, you create an adapter for that interface. For example, suppose you find that opening a buffered file in Java is a little complicated. You create a class MyFileInputStream that adapts that class. The interface for this class could look like the following:[5]

```
class MyFileInputStream
    {
    MyFileInputStream(Filename name) throws FileNotFoundDeviation,
        FileNotAccessibleDeviation, FileError
        { ...  }
    read() throws EndofFileDeviation, FileError
        {...}
    close()
        {...}
    //... Other methods,
    }
```

---

[5]This is a simple example of an adapter. You always have trade-offs in using an adapter class for library routines. A developer new to a project needs to learn a new class.

> ### A Textual Adapter
>
> Adapting interfaces is not limited to such programmatic interfaces. You can adapt textual interfaces. An example of adaptation is the sendmail configuration process. sendmail is a common email server. It uses the configuration file `sendmail.cf`. The syntax for that file is, well, to put it nicely, "interesting." To simplify configuration, there is a `sendmail.mc` file. The syntax of that file is in a macro language (m4). You transform `sendmail.mc` into `sendmail.cf` by using the m4 program.
>
> The `sendmail.mc` file represents a textual adapter. Now, people might suggest that the syntax of that file is still somewhat "interesting." But at least it's simpler than the `sendmail.cf` file.

The buffering is internal to this class. The methods signal a set of conditions that you find more meaningful than just IOException.[6] The close method does not throw an exception. The exception is caught within the adapter, which simplifies using the interface. If an exception occurs, it is logged.

ADAPTER

Advantage—you use an interface designed on your needs.

Disadvantage—adapting standard interfaces creates more interfaces to learn.

11.6 Façade

The Adapter pattern turns a single interface into a different interface. The Façade pattern turns multiple interfaces into a single interface. For example, the WeatherInformationTransformer interface in the Web Conglomerator solution (Chapter 9) hides the multiple interfaces of WeatherInformation, WeatherInformationDataGatherer, and WeatherInformationDisplayFormatter.

---

[6]I like to split errors into deviations (failures that may occur during normal operation of a program) and errors (failures that should not normally occur). For example, not having permission to read a file is something that could happen. A user could alter the permissions of the file and rerun the operation. An error reading from a file because of a hardware problem should never be normally encountered.

The user of WeatherInformationTransformer is not aware of the underlying interfaces.

FAÇADE

Advantage—a single interface can be easier to understand than multiples

11.7 Composite

In the Composite pattern, an interface to a group of objects is the same as that to a single object. The Composite pattern is commonly used with trees. A leaf on a tree has an interface. A branch (which has multiple leaves) has the same interface, plus an additional interface for adding or removing leaves. For example, the organization of a GUI usually works as a tree. The leaves are Components, and the branches are Containers:

```
interface Component
    draw()
interface ComponentContainer
    add_component(Component)
    remove_component(Component)
Widget implements Component
    draw()
Window implements ComponentContainer, Component
    draw()
    add_component(Component)
    remove_component(Component)
```

The draw() method for a Container such as Window invokes the draw() method for each of the Components it contains. Suppose a method receives a reference to a Component and wants to draw it. It does not matter whether the reference actually refers to a Widget or a Window. In either case, the method simply calls draw().

We can also use the Composite pattern to make a group of interfaces act like a single interface. For example, given the following interface:

```
interface StockTickerQuoter
    Dollar get_current_price(Ticker)
```

we could create an implementation that simply connects to a single source to provide the current price:

```
class StockTickerQuoterImplementation implements
    StockTickerQuoter
```

Alternatively, we could have an implementation that connects to multiple sources. It could average the prices from all sources, or it could call each source in turn until it found one that responded. The user's code would look the same, except for setting up the StockTickerQuoterContainer:

```
interface StockTickerQuoterContainer
    add(StockTickerQuoter)
    remove(StockTickerQuoter)
class StockTickerQuoterMultiple implements StockTickerQuoter,
    StockTickerQuoterContainer
```

A factory method can make using a composite like this transparent. Inside the method, StockTickerQuoter implementations can be added to StockTickerQuoterContainer. We might obtain an implementation with this:

```
enumeration StockTickerQuoterType = {
    FREE_BUT_DELAYED_SINGLE_SOURCE,
    PRICEY_BUT_CURRENT_SINGLE_SOURCE,
    AVERAGE_ALL_SOURCES};
StockTickerQuoter stock_ticker_quoter =
    StockTickerQuoterFactory.get_instance(AVERAGE_ALL_SOURCES)
```

COMPOSITE

> Advantage—calls to multiple implementations appear the same as calls to a single implementation

11.8 Things to Remember

We've looked at a number of patterns that deal with interfaces. These patterns are ways that multiple interfaces or multiple implementations can be opaque to the user. Employing these patterns can make your code more flexible and potentially easier to test.

- Factory Method
- Proxy
- Adapter
- Decorator
- Façade
- Composite

Appendix

You may be reading this because you didn't see the title "Appendix." Why is this material in an appendix? Well, it's "an accessory structure of the body" of the book. Some people might find particular topics in here that they think should have been part of the regular text. Just because the topics are in here doesn't mean they are not important; they just didn't fit into the flow. So, they got relegated to here.[1]

A.1 More about Document Style

We discussed document-style interfaces in Chapter 6. Here are a few more suggestions on how to employ them.

Document Suggestions

The XML Design ASC X12C Communications and Controls Committee compiled a number of suggestions for creating XML documents.[2] These suggestions can be useful, regardless of the actual form of the document. The suggestions include the following:

- Keep the use of features and choices to a minimum.

- Make the schema prescriptive: have schemas that are specific to a particular use, not generalized. More schemas make for fewer options, and thus you can have tighter validation.

- Limit randomness: have a limited number of variations.[3]

---

[1]And they really might not be that important to some people—that's OK; I won't be offended if you skip them.

[2]http://www.x12.org/x12org/xmldesign/X12Reference_Model_For_XML_Design.pdf

[3]The committee notes that limiting randomness provides a good philosophical basis for disallowing features such as substitution groups and the "ANY" content model when designing document schemas.

- Create reusable parts and context-sensitive parts. Examples of reusable parts are Addresses and Contact Information.

- Form a tree of compositions with optional and repetition specifiers

- Have a document version number. If changes have been made in the document, update the version number. (Or have a chain of unique IDs that reference previous versions.)

Using Standard Documents

If you are developing documents for internal use, you are free to develop your own forms. However, you may want to investigate the standards to avoid re-creating the wheel. Standard documents may have more data than you really need or desire, but they offer a good starting point for creating your own documents. For example, if you are developing a commerce system, investigate all the standard transaction sets of the federal government. These standards are being converted to XML (OASIS ebXML). If those sets do not make sense in your application, then search the Internet for ones that might be more appropriate.

To make use of the standards, set up a data interface (a DTO) that parallels the document structure. Use this interface to create the document with appropriate validation. For an example, let's use the Federal Information Processing Standards.[4] One of the standard documents for a purchase order is the FIPS 850 Purchase Order Transaction Set.[5] A data interface, such as the DTO given next, can represent this transaction set. We don't show the entire interface, since the specification for this transaction set is 262 pages long.[6] The specification is broken down into elements that have initials. The element initials are at the beginning of each name in the DTO. Normally the names in a DTO should not be tied to specific numbers. In this case, however, they are used to explicitly tie the fields to the specification.

```
data interface PurchaseOrderTransactionSet
    ST_TransactionSetHeader
        ST01_TransactionSetCode = 850
        String ST02_TransactionSetControlNumber
        enumeration PurposeCode {ORIGINAL, DUPLICATE, ...}
```

---

[4]See http://www.itl.nist.gov/fipspubs/ to get complete documents.

[5]See http://www.sba.gov/test/wbc/docs/procure/csystsba.html for an introductory description of the ASC X12 transaction sets.

[6]See http://fedebiz.disa.mil/FILE/IC/DOD/3010/R3010/R3010/Rev1/31r850_a.pdf.

```
enumeration POTypeCode {CONTRACT, GRANT...}
BEG_BeginningSegmentForPurchaseOrder
    PurposeCode BEG01_TransactionSetPurposeCode
    POTypeCode BEG02_PurchaseOrderTypeCode
    CommonString BEG03_PurchaseOrderNumber
    enumeration UnitCodes {EACH, FEET,...}
    PO1_baseline_item_data []
        String PO101_assigned_identification
        Count PO102_quantity_ordered
        UnitCodes PO103_unit_or_basis_for_measurement
        Money PO104_unit_price
```

Just creating the DTO may help you understand the organization of the document. You can build into this DTO checks for the rules for the transaction set. For simple validation, the set methods for each field can enforce the rules. An overall validation method can handle the cross-validation of fields.

Your internal document may not require all the fields listed in the specification. So just include the ones you need. If you need to convert your internal document to an external one that matches this specification, you'll find it easy to copy the corresponding fields.

A.2 Service-Oriented Architecture

Service-oriented architecture (SOA) is an emerging standard for providing remote services both to clients internal to an organization and to external organizations. Chances are you soon will communicate using SOA services. An SOA service is reusable, well-defined, published, and standards-compliant. An SOA service groups a set of operations, similar to the way that service interfaces, described in Chapter 2, group a set of methods. Like service interfaces and implementations, how an SOA service performs an operation is entirely opaque to a consumer of that service.

SOA operations tend to be business-oriented operations, such as the individual steps in the airline reservation example shown in Chapter 6, rather than technical operations, such as retrieving a database record. A business process uses a sequence of these operations to perform a particular action, such as the airline reservation process. Examining an enterprise for reusable services and creating an entire service-oriented architecture are beyond the scope of this book. Designing the services' contract and their protocol (sequence of operations or documents) is the essence of creating an SOA service. The same contractual and protocol design trade-offs that we have explored in this book for interfaces also apply to services. Services are effectively interfaces, albeit at a higher level.

SOA frameworks provide additional services beyond standards for documents and communication protocols that ensure interoperability. For example, they can offer security: encryption of communication, authentication (identification of a user), and authorization (determining that a user is entitled to perform specific operations). Using an SOA framework with its attendant services decreases the amount of time involved in creating an external interface.[7]

As this book is going to print, the Organization for the Advancement of Structured Information Standards (OASIS) is working on SOA standard models. Depending on your viewpoint, SOA uses either only message-based interfaces (document-style) or both message-based and Remote Procedure Call–based (procedural-style) interfaces. A general consensus says that an SOA must have the following characteristics:

- Interface is platform-independent (OS, language)—loosely coupled.
- Services are discoverable—dynamically locatable.
- Services are self-contained.

SOA frameworks such as web services and CORBA meet these characteristics. Some authors suggest another constraint:

- Service provider and consumer communicate via messages (i.e., a document-style interface)

In that case, CORBA would not be considered an SOA.

An SOA framework, mapped to web services and CORBA, is shown in Figure A.1, on the next page.

The PizzaOrdering document interchange shown in Chapter 6 can form the basis for a simple SOA service. Figure A.2, on the facing page shows how a service consumer connects to an implementation of a PizzaOrdering service. The consumer contacts the directory service and requests information about a host that provides an implementation of

---

[7]See http://www-128.ibm.com/developerworks/webservices/library/ws-soad1/ for more details about SOAs.

Feature	Web Services	CORBA
Service description	WSDL—Web Service Description Language	IDL
Service protocol	SOAP— Simple Object Access Protocol	IIOP—Internet Inter-Orb Protocol
Discovery of services	UDDI—Universal DIscovery, Description, and Integration	Directory Services
Platform independence mechanism	XML	Translation into local platform/language stub

Figure A.1: PIZZAORDERING SERVICE

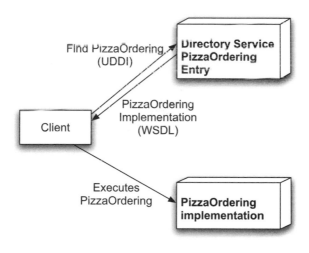

Figure A.2: PIZZAORDERING SERVICE

the interface. The consumer then contacts the implementation host and executes the protocol for the interface.

> ### JINI
>
> The JINI (Jini Is Not Initials) technology takes a different approach to making the platform and the protocol opaque. A client looks up a particular service, identified by a Java interface, in a JINI directory. When the client contacts a provider of that service, a Java implementation of the interface is downloaded to the client (thus providing platform independence). The client accesses the service through that implementation. The implementation may provide the service locally, or it may communicate with remote servers using any type of protocol (thus offering protocol opaqueness).
>
> The client needs to be programmed in Java, but the remote servers can be coded in any language.*
>
> ---
>
> *You can find more information at `http://www.artima.com/jini/jiniology/` and at `http://www.jini.org/`.

A.3 Collections and Collection Methods

Interfaces can decouple the use of data from the means used to store the data. We examine interface design that can be used for decoupling. We also explore Apple's innovative approach.

Suppose the pizza shop wants to keep track of orders for its pizzas. You have three elements: the Pizza, the Customer, and the Order. An Order represents the order by a Customer for a Pizza. You might come up with the following classes, which represent data interfaces:

```
class Pizza
    Toppings []
    Size

class Customer
    Address
    Name

class Order
    Customer
    Pizza
```

Now the Orders are going to be kept in a collection somewhere. The collection could be a database, an XML file, or a comma-delimited file. In any event, the interface to the collection should be the same. The use of the collection should not be coupled to the implementation for the collection.[8] The interface may look like this:

```
interface OrderCollection
    Order [] find_orders_containing_toppings(Toppings [])
    Order [] find_orders_for_customer(Customer)
    Order [] find_order_by_size(Size)
```

Now how about finding all orders placed by customers who lived more than five miles away? You might as well make the method a little more general:

```
Order [] find_orders_from_customers_at_distances (Distance minimum,
Distance maximum)
```

With a little switch in the interface design, we can allow for ANDs and ORs of criteria. Instead of the find methods returning an array of Orders, they could return an OrderCollection:

```
interface OrderCollection
    OrderCollection find_orders_containing_toppings(Toppings [])
    OrderCollection find_orders_for_customer(Customer)
    OrderCollection find_order_by_size(Size)
    OrderCollection merge(OrderCollection)
    OrderCollection oc = new OrderCollectionImplementation();
```

Then we can apply a sequence of method calls to further select (i.e., do an AND) from a returned OrderCollection. For example:

```
OrderCollection selection = oc.find_orders_for_customer(a_customer).
    find_order_by_size(size)
```

The merge allows an ORing opportunity. You can take the results from two different finds and merge them.

If you start using complex search criteria, then you may want to split the responsibilities for the collection. You can separate the matching criteria from the find. For example:

```
interface OrderCollection
    Order [] find_orders(callback_selection_method)
```

The callback_selection() method determines whether a particular Order should be included in the output. This is the push version of going through a collection.

---

[8]Let me state that this statement is probably one of the most controversial in this book. So, you may be on the other side and have a strong opinion on it. Just consider this a look at the dark side.

```
Boolean this_order_matches(Order current_order)
    {
    //Return true if the order meets your criteria
    }
```

With this organization, you can make up more matching criteria without having to alter the OrderCollection class. However, we force going through the collection on an element-by-element basis. If you have an SQL database underneath, you may want to have this callback return a WHERE clause that can be added to the query. For example:[9]

```
String orders_by_size(Size size)
    {
    return "SIZE = " + size;
    }
```

If you put all the different methods in the collection as in the first version, it becomes a more complete interface (see Chapter 4), which is simple to use. But its completeness may be a turn-off to some users. You could provide the simple interface as in the second version (which is what most collections do with predicates). You could then add the first as a complete interface that calls the second one, for users who like simplicity.

Web Conglomerator

In the Web Conglomerator example, we hinted that you could write a configuration GUI that allows the user to alter which InformationTransformers are displayed. You can use a collection class (regular or template) from a language library to hold this collection. You may want to create a specific interface to that collection that adds specific methods.

In creating a user interface, we found that we missed an important data element. Each InformationTransformer needs a name that can be displayed to the user:

```
interface InformationTransformer
    String display_name
    gather_data_for_location(Location)
        signals DataUnavailable
    String format_for_html_display()
```

---

[9]This is an outstanding example where you cannot have completely opaque interfaces, especially when performance is critical.

Predicates

Apple's Mac OS X application framework is called Cocoa;* part of Cocoa uses predicates to encode queries in an manner independent of the backing store (e.g., the database). The predicates are a filtering mechanism. They can be simple comparisons (`age > 30`), case-insensitive matches (`name contains[smith]`), and logical operations (AND, OR, NOT).

A predicate query is translated into whatever language is required by the backing store (e.g., SQL, XML). The predicates do not provide all possible queries that a particular backing store can support. On the other hand, they represent a larger set of queries than some backing stores support. In the documentation, Apple notes, "Not all possible predicate queries are supported by all backing stores.... When constructing predicates, you should take care that they will work with your data store. The back end may downgrade the predicate (for example It may make a case-sensitive comparison case-insensitive) or raise an exception if you try to use an unsupported operator."

Microsoft also has a similar project underway, as part of the .NET framework, called .NET Language Integrated Query (LINQ).[†].

---

*Thanks to Keith Ray for bringing Cocoa to my attention. See `http://developer.apple.com/documentation/Cocoa/Conceptual/Predicates/index.html`.

[†]`http://msdn.microsoft.com/netframework/future/linq/default.aspx?pull=/library/en-us/dndotnet/html/linqprojectovw.asp`

We can display the list of names so that the user can select and unselect items for display, as well as add and delete InformationTransformers. Working through the possibilities yields an interface like this:

```
interface LocationInformationTransformerCollection
    String [] get_names_of_selected_for_display()
    String [] get_names_of_all()
    LocationInformationTransformers [] get_selected_for_display()
    LocationInformationTransformers [] get_all()
    add(LocationInformationTransformer)
    remove(index)
    select_for_display(index)
    unselect_for_display(index)
    set_order_for_display(index, order)
    store()
    load()
```

This interface doe not specify how the collection is stored. You could convert the data to text, save it with Java serialization, or use a database. This interface is more complete (see Chapter 4), which makes it simpler to use.

How to design the GUI interface that manipulates this collection is left to other design books.

A.4   Configuration

Configuration was mentioned in a sidebar in Chapter 7. You may wonder how you get an implementation of the Configuration interface. You could have a factory method. At some point, you'll need the Singleton pattern (see *Design Patterns*) either as a class or as a method. Whether you use a separate class or simply have a classwide (static) method is up to you. For example:

```
class ConfigurationFactory
    static Configuration getConfiguration();
```

or

```
class ConfiguratonFactory
    static ConfigurationFactory getInstance();
  Configuration getConfiguration();
```

In either case, an instance of Configuration is returned. The Configuration interface listed in the chapter had only get methods. You can also have set methods. The configuration values could be set with a stateful-looking or stateless-looking interface (see Chapter 3):

```
interface Configuration
    set_pizza_toppings(Topping [] toppings);
```

or

```
interface Configuration
    add_pizza_topping(Topping topping);
    clear_pizza_toppings();
```

You could also create a generic configuration interface:

```
set_item_value(String name, String value)
String get_item_value(String item_name)
```

In this case, you do not have type checking on the configuration values. The user needs to ensure that the configuration values are valid (just like with the document-style remote interface in Chapter 6). On retrieval the user has to convert the values back into the appropriate data types.

Configuration and Factories

A particular place where configuration can occur is when using a factory. The actual implementation that is returned from a factory is opaque to the caller; it simply implements the required interface. The factory needs to decide what implementation to return. In some instances, you might want the factory to return a test Implementation, and in other instances, you might want it to return the production version. You could make this selection in two ways.

First, the factory could access a configuration mechanism that indicated which implementation to return. Second, the factory could have additional methods for setting its configuration.[10] These methods would not necessarily be called by the caller. Instead, the caller would ask a configuration mechanism to return a factory that is configured appropriately. (Swing is an example of this mechanism.)

Now we get into one more level of indirection. The factory itself hides the implementation. Then instead of simply accessing a singleton factory, we first create a factory that has the appropriate configuration and then use it to return an appropriate implementation.

A.5 Another Service Registry Iteration

For those who didn't think two iterations were enough, here are the features for a third one.

Matching Criteria

We can't stop coming up with new ideas for the Service Registry in Chapter 10. Here's yet another one with possible changes to the interfaces. What is interesting about this feature is that the decision of assigning responsibility for implementing the feature has substantial ramifications. Whatever you scratch on your IRI cards as the responsible interface is probably bound to change.

---

[10]This is the Dependency Injection pattern (also called Inversion of Control). See http://www.martinfowler.com/articles/injection.html for a discussion of this pattern.

We briefly discussed the case of having hundreds of ServiceProviders offer the same ServiceID. One way to avoid returning a large number of ServiceProviders is to establish a mechanism for selecting a smaller number. For example, a ServiceConsumer may want to select a ServiceProvider based on criteria other than just providing a service. The ServiceProvider could supply some details, such as the skill level of the player (for an interactive game), location information, or any other information that a ServiceConsumer might want to use in selecting a ServiceProvider. We cannot think of all the possible criteria, so we just create a DetailInformation field that will contain the criteria. A particular service determines how information in that field is used for matching.

Matching could take place in two places. The client could get the DetailInformation for all ServiceProviders and then wade through them to find desired matches in whatever manner is desired. That can place a burden on the Service Registry to return lots of matches. Alternatively, the criteria could be matched in the Service Registry. That seems to be a bit more work for the Service Registry, but it can substantially decrease the number of ConnectionInformations that are returned.

You are often faced with similar trade-offs in communicating over the network. The server can perform more internal processing and cut down on the communication between the client and the server, or vice versa. The choice is dependent on the relative time and cost differences between processing and communicating.

The document interface will be different in the two cases, but the ServiceConsumer interface will almost be the same. We add DetailInformation to ServiceProviderInformation. Since we are performing matching on the server, then we need to add MatchCriteria to the LookupRequest. The interfaces for ServiceConsumer and ServiceProvider change slightly:

```
interface ServiceConsumer
    ConnectionInformation [] lookup_service(UUID service_id,
        MatchCriteria match_criteria, Authorization authorization)
            signals UnableToConnect, StatusFailure
interface ServiceProvider
    register_service(UUID service_id, UUID server_id,
        TimePeriod time_to_live,
        ConnectionInformation connect_info, DetailInformation
detail_information,
        Authorization authorization)  signals UnableToConnect,
        StatusFailure
    unregister_service(UUID service_id, UUID server_id,
        ConnectionInformation connect_info) signals UnableToConnect,
StatusFailure
```

We haven't specified the details for MatchCriteria. We're pretty sure it will have "contains" matching. There are other possibilities, such as regular expression matching or wildcard matching. We'll leave those details until we check with our user base and also determine the processing requirements.

A.6 Other Interface Issues

Here's a few more ideas on various topics. Consider this an appendix to the appendix

Forcing Interfaces Together

You may want to generalize interfaces into a common interface. We didn't do that with the InformationTransformers in Chapter 9, but just considered them as a framework. In Chapter 3, we introduced the IceCreamOrdering interface. We presented the PizzaOrdering interface in Chapter 1. These interfaces have different methods. We could rework them so that they appear as a single interface. For example, we could have the following:

```
interface OrderItem
    specify_options()
interface Order
    order_item(OrderItem)
IceCream implements OrderItem
    specify_options()
        // Ask for and sets cone type
        // and flavors
Pizza implements OrderItem
    specify_options()
        // Ask for and sets size and toppings
```

Mixins

The Ruby language features (among other things) mixins. These are modules that can be included in a class definition. The methods in a mixin act as anonymous base classes. The methods get added to the methods defined in the class. For example, the Comparable mixin adds the comparison operators <, < =, ==, >=, and > to a class. However, the Comparable module relies on the presence of the <=> operator in the class in which it is included. This operator compares two objects and returns -1, 0, or +1, which represents the object's definition of less than, equal, and greater than. The Comparable module calls that operator to implement the other comparison operators.

The need for this operator is documented in the description of Comparable. Executing one of the operators without having defined the <=> operator results in a runtime error, not a compile-time error, since Ruby does not have explicit typing. One could document the need for the <=> operator by saying that a module must implement an interface as follows:

```
interface Comparison
    operator <=> (another)
```

If this same method was needed by other mixins or by other code, creating an interface makes the common need more explicit.

Composition over Inheritance

This is another example of the benefits of composition over inheritance, in case you haven't been convinced.[11] Suppose you build an application for a veterinarian. Suppose that you create a hierarchy with Pet as the base class and Cats, Dogs, and Birds as derived classes with different data for each. An attribute of Pet is Owner.

When the Discovery Channel calls and asks you to build a system to help keep track of their animal documentaries, you cannot reuse that animal domain, because that domain is hardwired to have all animal types with "owners" and be classified as Pets.

A pet is a role an animal plays, not a special kind of animal. Roles are best modeled with composition. Had your original animal domain allowed for the animal to have a role object (or perhaps a set of roles), you could now have a role for Pet, a role for DocumentarySubject, and so on, leveraging the domain model you already had. (However, trying to design for ultimate reuse ends up creating a system with so many abstraction layers that the rubber can never meet the road.)

---

[11]David Bock supplied this example.

Index

Competitive Edge

Practices of an Agile Developer

Agility for individuals. See the personal habits, ideas, and approaches of successful agile software developers. • Learn how to improve your software development process • See what real agile practices feel like • Keep agile practices in balance • Avoid the common temptations that kill projects • Harness the power of continuous development

Practices of an Agile Developer: Working in the Real World
Venkat Subramaniam and Andy Hunt
(200 pages) ISBN: 0-9745140-8-X. $29.95

Ship It!

Agility for teams. The next step from the individual focus of *Practices of an Agile Developer* is the team approach that let's you *Ship It!*, on time and on budget, without excuses. You'll see how to implement the common technical infrastructure that every project needs along with well-accepted, easy-to-adopt, best-of-breed practices that really work, as well as common problems and how to solve them.

Ship It!: A Practical Guide to Successful Software Projects
Jared Richardson and Will Gwaltney
(200 pages) ISBN: 0-9745140-4-7. $29.95

Cutting Edge

Learn how to use the popular Ruby programming language from the Pragmatic Programmers: your definitive source for reference and tutorials on the Ruby language and exciting new application development tools based on Ruby.

The *Facets of Ruby* series includes the definitive guide to Ruby, widely known as the PickAxe book, and *Agile Web Development with Rails*, the first and best guide to the cutting-edge Ruby on Rails application framework.

Programming Ruby (The PickAxe)

The definitive guide to Ruby programming.
• Up-to-date and expanded for Ruby version 1.8. • Complete documentation of all the built-in classes, modules, methods, and standard libraries. • Learn more about Ruby's web tools, unit testing, and programming philosophy.

Programming Ruby: The Pragmatic Programmer's Guide, 2nd Edition
Dave Thomas with Chad Fowler
and Andy Hunt
(864 pages) ISBN: 0-9745140-5-5. $44.95

Agile Web Development with Rails

A new approach to rapid web development.
Develop sophisticated web applications quickly and easily • Learn the framework of choice for Web 2.0 developers • Use incremental and iterative development to create the web apps that users want • Get to go home on time.

Agile Web Development with Rails: A Pragmatic Guide
Dave Thomas and David Heinemeier Hansson
(570 pages) ISBN: 0-9766940-0-X. $34.95

Visit our secure online store: http://pragmaticprogrammer.com/catalog

The Pragmatic Bookshelf

The Pragmatic Bookshelf features books written by developers for developers. The titles continue the well-known Pragmatic Programmer style, and continue to garner awards and rave reviews. As development gets more and more difficult, the Pragmatic Programmers will be there with more titles and products to help programmers stay on top of their game.

Visit Us Online

Interface-Oriented Design
pragmaticprogrammer.com/titles/kpiod
Errata, and other resources. Come give us feedback, too!

Register for Updates
pragmaticprogrammer.com/updates
Be notified when updates and new books become available.

Join the Community
pragmaticprogrammer.com/community
Read our weblogs, join our online discussions, participate in our mailing list, interact with our wiki, and benefit from the experience of other Pragmatic Programmers.

New and Noteworthy
pragmaticprogrammer.com/news
Check out the latest pragmatic developments in the news.

Save on the PDF

Save on the PDF version of this book. Owning the paper version of this book entitles you to purchase the PDF version at a deep discount. The PDF is great for carrying around on your laptop. It's hyperlinked, has color, and is fully searchable. Buy it now at pragmaticprogrammer.com/coupon

Contact Us

Phone Orders:	1-800-699-PROG (+1 919 847 3884)
Online Orders:	www.pragmaticprogrammer.com/catalog
Customer Service:	support@pragmaticprogrammer.com
Non-English Versions:	translations@pragmaticprogrammer.com
Pragmatic Teaching:	academic@pragmaticprogrammer.com
Author Proposals:	proposals@pragmaticprogrammer.com